THE TAO OF TRADING

THE TAO OF TRADING

HOW TO BUILD ABUNDANT WEALTH

IN ANY MARKET CONDITION

SIMON REE

HOUNDSTOOTH
PRESS

THE TAO OF TRADING

How to Build Abundant Wealth in Any Market Condition

ISBN   978-1-5445-0817-7   *Hardcover*

978-1-5445-0816-0   *Paperback*

978-1-5445-0815-3   *Ebook*

This book is dedicated to everyone out there who is giving trading a shot. To anyone who wants to beat Wall Street at its own game. To all the people who are rising above the haters and doing something most people say can't be done. Power to every one of you!

CONTENTS

INTRODUCTION

The world has changed in the last thirty years, and with it, the way markets operate.

Thirty years ago, the most successful investors in the world had the biggest funnels of information. Today, the best investors have the best *filters* of information.

Our access to free, virtually instant information can be both a blessing and a curse for the aspiring investor. The market is filled with opportunities and opinions. Swimming in this ocean of information, it is an increasingly difficult task for investors to filter the noise and find the signal.

It is often difficult for the individual investor to discern whether the information they are receiving is low-quality, biased, or agenda-driven. Acting upon such information can lead to significant financial mishaps.

I wrote this book to help you:

- Understand how the financial markets and Wall Street *really* work
- Become knowledgeable and confident enough to make your own trading decisions
- Navigate the markets in such a way that you can be profitable whether the stock market is rising or falling
- Filter the noise and find the signal, so you can focus only on what really matters when it comes to trading the markets

It is a difficult environment for anyone following conventional wisdom when it comes to investing. Let me explain what I mean.

Let's look for a moment at stocks and bonds: the two cornerstones of any traditional investment portfolio.

The stock market is as expensive as it has ever been according to many experts, as well as some highly regarded measures of stock market valuation. As I write this, the S&P 500 and Nasdaq are at all-time highs and Warren Buffett's favorite stock market valuation tool* is also at an all-time high.

"Value investing" hasn't worked for well over a decade. Most investors—professionals included—have failed to adapt to the way the investing game is now being played, in an environment where central banks are buying up trillions of dollars' worth of assets each year.

Bonds, too, are expensive relative to history. The yields offered by bonds range from paltry to negative. As of November 2019, there

---

* Total market capitalization to Gross Domestic Product (GDP) is widely regarded as Warren Buffett's preferred gauge of stock market valuation. As of this writing, the ratio is at 153 percent, an all-time high.

were approximately $13 trillion worth of bonds in existence globally that trade with a negative yield. This is unprecedented!

(A bond with a negative yield is a bond that you are guaranteed to lose money on if you hold it until maturity. Most people would agree that this doesn't make for a particularly attractive investment.)

WHAT IS AN INDIVIDUAL INVESTOR TO DO?

So, if you're a baby boomer facing retirement (the median age of baby boomers in 2019 was sixty-five) what are you to do? How are you going to earn an income in retirement? Money in the bank pays you nothing, returns available in the bond market are paltry, so the only game in town is the stock market...right?

Well...there's a problem with that "solution." The big question with piling your life's savings in the stock market when you are facing retirement is: what is likely to happen to your life's savings when the next recession comes around?

The stock market is likely to fall 30 percent to 50 percent. It's just what stock markets do during recessions; we've seen this movie before. If you're a retiree with a stock portfolio and the thought of this doesn't send a shiver down your spine, then you're made of granite!

When you're a retiree and your employment income stops, you can no longer "buy the dip" when stocks fall. In fact, you're much more likely to be in a rush to preserve whatever money you have left in the market—which may mean rapidly selling all your stocks when (or more likely, well after) the next recessions hits.

The picture is only marginally more favorable for millennials. Property prices in many cities around the world are vastly beyond the reach of this generation, many of whom have postponed—or given up altogether—the dream of home ownership.

The stock market today isn't a particularly attractive destination for investment given the valuation concerns. And bonds are not an attractive proposition given the very low-to-negative yields on offer. Property prices in many major cities around the world are trading at valuations that are well above historical averages.

Everything you might want to invest in looks expensive! So, what is a retiree to do if they want to earn an income while preserving their wealth? What is a millennial to do if they want to grow their wealth rapidly?

SOME GOOD NEWS AND SOME BAD NEWS

Now let me share with you some good news and some bad news.

The good news is that, armed with the information and insights contained in this very book—together with a little consistent effort—you will have the knowledge to be able to:

- Navigate the stock market with confidence
- Become a profitable trader no matter whether the stock market is rising or falling
- Earn the type of consistent positive returns from the stock market that would seem impossible to somebody without this knowledge

- Know exactly when you should pull the trigger—or pull the plug—on an investment
- Manage your risk like a professional, so that you can sleep well at night
- Generate a consistent second income from the stock market—or even make it your full-time income one day

Does this sound good or *good*?

OK, so what's the bad news?

Well, the bad news is that it is largely going to come down to your own efforts.

If you want to:

- Grow your wealth rapidly and consistently
- Be profitable whether markets are rising or falling
- Make good investment decisions without having to listen to stock market research, mainstream news media, or financial newsletters

You cannot outsource the management of your entire investment capital[†] to a bank, broker, investment adviser, "robo-adviser," or any other player in the investment advice industry. You must assume this responsibility yourself. We will explore exactly why this is the case in chapter one.

---

† Capital simply means *money*. It is one of the words people in the finance industry use to make themselves sound smarter.

WHAT I'M NOT SUGGESTING

If you currently use someone for financial advice and you are happy with them, I am NOT suggesting that upon reading this book, you fire them and start doing it all yourself.

Let me be very clear on that!

A more sensible approach would be to start employing the methods you will learn in this book on a small amount of your investment capital. As your ability and confidence grows, start allocating more capital to the money you are managing yourself and watch as your account balloons.

If you are new to investing and you have some surplus cash sitting idly that you can afford to put at risk, the methods in this book could be the perfect place for you to get started.

I applaud you for taking this important step to secure your financial freedom and I welcome you on this trading journey.

CHAPTER 1

UNCONVENTIONAL WISDOM

"Never accept ultimatums, conventional wisdom, or absolutes."

—CHRISTOPHER REEVE

"...the only way to get ahead is to find errors in conventional wisdom."

—LARRY ELLISON

"When you're used to being prepared to reject conventional wisdom, it leaves you open to learn more."

—MAYIM BIALIK, PHD

The financial markets are the number one place on earth for anyone wanting to create extra income and grow their wealth. The opportunity set is enormous, and you won't have to pay a lot in overheads or tie money up in illiquid assets.

The benefits of trading are almost too numerous to mention. As a trader, you won't have a boss telling you what to do. You won't have to ask somebody else's permission to take a day off or have a holiday.

You won't have to hire any staff either. Managing staff can be an overwhelming task for many small businesses.

Your start-up costs will be small, compared with almost any other business venture you might contemplate.

You won't have to deal with complaining customers who don't pay on time. You won't have to negotiate with hard-ass suppliers who are trying to screw you down for every last dollar.

You'll never have to sit through endless performance reviews or sales meetings, for an organization that would sack you in a heart-beat if that action was deemed to be in the best interests of some faceless shareholders.

Trading is enormously empowering. It offers you the potential for incredible freedom. The biggest problem many successful traders face is what to do with the other twenty-three hours of their day that are not spent trading!

As a trader, you live or die by your own efforts. This is brilliant news for people prepared to spend the time acquiring the proper education and mindset. There is a strong chance that you are just such a person, because you are reading this book. Congratulations and welcome, I look forward to guiding you on your trading journey!

Every aspiring trader knows deep inside that if they could just "crack the code" of the financial markets and learn to trade consistently in any market condition, they would have the keys to the abundance they deserve.

But without proper information and guidance, the financial markets can seem like a maze at best, and like a minefield at worst. "Cracking the code" is tough!

I have spent the better part of the last twenty years cracking that code myself, and I've written this book with the purpose of helping you successfully trade the stock market, whether it is rising or falling. I want you to not just survive, but prosper through all the economic booms and busts that lie in our future.

In 2017, I decided to leave the finance industry, where I had spent the previous twenty-five years of my life. I had spent well over a decade in a dealing room, staring at a Bloomberg terminal for ten to twelve hours a day. This may not sound thrilling...and believe me, most of the time it wasn't. But spending that much time learning how financial markets operate, afforded me the opportunity to educate myself on how to trade the markets.

I also had the privilege of working alongside some of the smartest people and some of the best professional traders in the finance industry. Not only that, I have worked with and consulted to some of the wealthiest and most successful families and businesspeople across Asia and Australia. The opportunity to learn from these people has been invaluable in my journey.

I learned about how trends form, how they persist, and how price typically responds under certain circumstances. And, I have figured out ways to exploit this price action for profit.

In my twenty-five-year career as a banker, adviser, and player in the markets, I have witnessed firsthand the many hurdles individual investors and traders face. I have developed methods to help people overcome these hurdles in order to be successful.

With this book I seek to empower you with the skills, knowledge, and techniques necessary to maximize your profit potential while teaching you how to minimize risk. My desire is that you will be able to trade the markets consistently while sleeping well at night.

WHAT TO EXPECT FROM THIS BOOK

The title of this book was inspired by *The Tao of Jeet Kune Do* by Bruce Lee. In addition to being a trader, I am also a Jeet Kune Do instructor and I perceive some important parallels between martial arts and trading. Martial arts are not just about punching, kicking, and grappling. These aspects are important, but what powers the physical aspects of a martial art to victory? The engine behind it all is your mindset, your psychology, your will to win. Many martial artists have great technique, but maybe they can't take a hit. When they do take a hit, their mindset collapses, their engine stops, and their techniques just don't have the drive anymore. Similarly, trading is not all about entries, exits, and reading indicators. These are important, but what powers a trader to victory is her mindset, her psychology, her will to win. Most aspiring traders just don't have the right mindset, which makes trading success elusive.

This is not your traditional book of Tao. Neither is this a traditional trading textbook. This book is called *The Tao of Trading* because Tao means "the way." And in my own unconventional, tongue-in-cheek style, this book will teach you "the way" to build abundant wealth regardless of the market circumstances you find yourself in. This book is the culmination of my twenty-five years of experience trading the markets, and it will help you acquire both the techniques and the mindset you need to be successful in trading. It is the very information I wish someone had shared with me when I commenced my journey as a trader.

UNCONVENTIONAL WISDOM

If all mankind ever did was adhere to conventional wisdom, we would still believe that the earth was flat and that the sun revolves around the earth. Progress would be almost impossible.

In order to progress, we must always be prepared to question and challenge conventional wisdom.

Finance, in particular, is a field where conventional wisdom can really trip you up, or at least lead you to some less-than-stellar results. Unfortunately, finance is also a field where it is casually dispensed as though it was absolute fact.

I wrote this book because trading the financial markets can be a lucrative and empowering profession that grants enormous freedom to those who become good at it. But very few truly manage to get good at trading.

Trade setups, knowing when to pull the trigger on a trade, and knowing when to take profit are all important aspects of trading, and I will teach you a simple, time-tested, high probability setup in this book that you can start using straight away.

But there are even more important aspects to trading that most aspiring traders aren't aware of. Many traders literally don't know what they don't know in this regard. If, as a new trader, you only focus on indicators and setups, your failure is virtually assured. Becoming a successful trader requires an open mind and genuine curiosity. In the following pages of this book, I will share stories and anecdotes with you that I hope will not just entertain you, but spark your curiosity and inspire you to question some of what you think you know about the financial markets. I'm going to strip back some of the conventional wisdom that pervades the finance industry and prepare you for a more unconventional—and profitable—approach. Prepare to keep an open mind!

I encourage you to read this book in order, starting with this chapter, then progressing through chapters 2 to 14 in sequence. Each new chapter will build upon information you learned in the previous chapter. Skipping ahead will be less rewarding!

In the remainder of **chapter 1**, I will take you on a brief backstage tour of Wall Street. You will learn why as an individual investor, you should not turn to Wall Street "solutions" if your goal is to grow your wealth quickly.

In **chapter 2**, we will explore the five big myths of Wall Street together. You will learn how these myths are holding you back from your full wealth creation potential.

Chapter 3 discusses why trading is like sex. In completing this chapter, you will start to develop a successful trader's mindset.

Ever heard of trend following? I call it the "ninth wonder of the world," and you will learn why in **chapter 4**. Once you have learned these principles, you will find making money in the markets becomes much easier.

In **chapter 5** we will take a deeper dive into reading price action, with lots of graphical examples. By the end of this chapter you will know whether you should be looking to buy, sell, or avoid a stock within seconds of looking at its price chart.

The concept of support and resistance is introduced in **chapter 6**, where I explain how and why price tends to get "stuck." This knowledge will help you identify great places to enter and exit your trades.

Chapter 7 introduces the concept of mean reversion, referred to by the legendary John C Bogle as "*the iron law of the financial markets.*" I will teach you how to use this *iron law* to benefit your trading.

In **chapter 8** I introduce you to options, by far my favorite trading instrument and what I trade personally. I have traded pretty much everything over the years, but options' trading is always at the core of what I do. You will learn how options offer *limited downside and unlimited upside*, which makes them a unique and flexible trading instrument. The powerful knowledge contained in this chapter alone is worth the cover price of this book.

I will share with you a simple yet powerful trading setup in **chapter 9**. This is a time-tested, high probability setup that works in both rising and falling markets. It's a setup that I developed and use personally and it's one of my favorite setups. You'll be up-and-running in no time after reading this chapter.

Chapter 10 goes into some detail about how to laser-target the highest probability setups. In this chapter you will learn my weeding-out process for assessing potential trades, step-by-step. As a result, you will have a greater edge on every trade you take.

In **chapter 11** we go slightly beyond the basics. In this chapter you will learn how to construct an option spread. This will enable you to further control your risk on a trade.

Chapter 12 is one of the most important chapters in the book. This chapter teaches you how to manage risk like a professional. This will be your key to success in trading the financial markets. I'll also share with you one of my more sordid war stories...

My step-by-step process for trading is outlined in detail in **Chapter 13**. This chapter will tie together everything you have learned so far in the book.

In **chapter 14** I will give you some tips on how to make this all happen. How to make the shift from a new trader or unprofitable trader, to a trader who is consistently profitable. We will also explore just what might be possible for you as a trader, once you start getting good. Don't miss this important chapter!

Now, I have booked you on a special "backstage tour" of Wall Street with me as your guide. You are about to learn why Wall Street is not the place to go to for help, if you are an individual investor looking to grow your wealth quickly.

A BACKSTAGE TOUR OF WALL STREET

If you are already very wealthy and your main goal is to preserve your wealth, Wall Street has got you covered. Those firms can do a great job of this.

However, Wall Street firms are not well positioned to service smaller investors who are looking to grow their wealth rapidly.

I want to highlight a couple of truths that inhibit Wall Street from being able to deliver strong investment performance to individual investors. They are:

1. A misalignment in objectives
2. The issue of scale

MISALIGNMENT IN OBJECTIVES

Let's talk about the misalignment in objectives first.

The key objectives of Wall Street and most financial advice firms are to:

- Convince wealthy people who have money to invest, to let the firm look after their money
- Charge a fee for looking after that money
- Not get sued in the process

When I refer to these as the "key" objectives of Wall Street firms, remember this: generating an acceptable return for business shareholders/owners ultimately drives the culture and behavior of employees in Wall Street firms.

Don't get me wrong. No honest player in the finance industry wants their clients to have a bad outcome. Particularly, an outcome their clients could potentially sue them for!

But there are misalignments in incentives and in culture that are rife throughout the industry.

The investment advice industry as a whole, does not pay its employees more if their clients make more money (i.e., if their clients earn better investment returns).

No, the client-facing employees of the industry—the private bankers, investment advisers and so forth—are only incentivized to onboard new clients, open accounts, increase the amount of money they look after (known as AUM, or assets under management), and entice clients to engage in transactions with them.

In terms of financial incentive, ensuring that the interests of their employer are taken care of offers significantly greater reward than ensuring that their clients' portfolios perform well.

Let me share with you a small sample of personal experiences that I hope will serve as a cautionary tale for you. These are all true stories—actual events that I witnessed firsthand!

"F*ck the clients!"

It was mid-2007. The general public—and most in the finance industry—was oblivious to the impending financial calamity. Stocks were flying high and so was confidence in all things financial.

At the time, I was heavily involved in determining suitable investment products to offer to some of the bank's wealthiest clients. Many of these products were manufactured by the investment bank and contained an eye-watering level of hidden fees. I opposed a great many investment products where investment payoff didn't make sense, or where the fee structure was highly disadvantageous to clients. I took my role in protecting clients' interests—and our franchise—very seriously.

Certain members of the investment bank had been strenuously lobbying to get my team to distribute CDOs to our wealthy clients and family offices. (CDOs are collateralized debt obligations—some of the most toxic types of mortgage-backed securities offered to clients before the global financial crisis). I repeatedly refused to let these products get anywhere near our clients. This was not a popular decision with my investment bank colleagues, since CDOs were literally fee-generating machines for the investment bank. This put me in conflict with some *very* senior people within the bank.

Then came along some "commodities-linked, structured, reverse-airbag bonus certificate" the investment bank wanted my team to distribute to clients. I forget the exact name of the product, but it was something equally absurd. Structured products with this level of convolution and complexity were quite common at the time. Trying to work out the circumstances that would have to transpire in order for a client to make money was quite the task!

I'll never forget the conversation I had with a very senior department head—known in the industry by the crude term *big swinging dick* ("BSD")—in the bank about this product. The exchange went like this:

BSD: "Simon, we want you to distribute this product."

Me: "No ####, I don't think this product is right for us."

BSD: "What do you mean, Simon? What's wrong with this product?"

Me: "Well ####, as always I'm concerned about the interests of our clients."

BSD: "(imitating me) 'What about the clients?' What *about* the clients? All I ever hear from you is 'what about the clients?' Well I'm here to say F*CK the clients! We're going to do things MY way from now on!"

I'm pleased to say that—despite the bluster—the product in question never saw the light of day. But this conversation was with a *very* senior member of the investment bank and a culture carrier of the firm.

It was at this point that I started to feel pretty jaded about my place of employment, if not yet about the industry. I was subsequently headhunted for a role with a different bank in Singapore that I accepted quite eagerly.

"You're not an adviser, you're a salesman!"

Sadly, my jaded attitude towards the finance industry didn't receive a boost after my move to another bank in Singapore. I had been at my new bank only a few weeks when I heard the head of the department yell across the dealing room floor, "You're not an adviser, you're a salesman!" This was directed at a colleague who was trying to make up his mind about whether an investment product was suitable for one of his clients.

This was a sentiment—and a refrain—that would reveal itself often. Sometimes subtly and sometimes obviously, as in the example above.

From my observation, this is a culture that is quite common across Wall Street firms. Clients, when presented with an investment product by their adviser, will often—and quite naturally—assume that the product has their adviser's endorsement. Otherwise, why would the adviser present it to them in the first place?

But as far as the Wall Street banks are concerned, the adviser's job is to sell investment products to clients rather than give investment advice to clients. According to the banks, the adviser is fulfilling her role in presenting the product to clients, regardless of whether she thinks it's suitable to her clients' needs. Remember too, that an adviser's performance and pay is going to be assessed on whether she makes money for the bank, not on whether she makes money for her clients.

"You eat what you kill!"

Late in 2016 I moved back to Australia for personal reasons. Before moving back, I was headhunted by some of the biggest international banks that have a presence in Australia. I went through several rounds of meetings to try and determine a good cultural fit.

I want to share with you a key takeaway from one particular conversation that will be forever etched into my memory.

I was meeting in Sydney with the Australian CEO of a global investment bank. A bank that employs hundreds of advisers across Australia and looks after tens of thousands of clients.

I was asking a question about the bank's business model, when the CEO answered, "Well you see Simon, we run a business model here where, you eat what you kill!"

Client fees were the "kill." "Eating" referred to the share of those fees his advisers would receive in commissions. And these words were straight from the lips of the country's CEO of a major global investment bank! I almost ran out of the office after that meeting. The exchange was enough to make me head back to my apartment to take a shower.

THE ISSUE OF SCALE

Cultural and financial misalignments aside, there is a more practical factor that impedes Wall Street from delivering great results for investors. The issue of scale.

A successful salesperson in the investment advice industry aspires to look after as many clients and as much AUM (money) as possible. This is how they can generate the maximum amount of fees... which ultimately determines what they get paid (and therefore, what they are incentivized to do). This is how they will earn more money to provide for their family, so it understandably becomes their main objective.

But if you're a financial adviser with 50, 100, 500, 1,000 clients... how much time can you really dedicate to each client's portfolio?

And when you are incentivized to attract new clients, open accounts, and manage more AUM, how much time do you even *want* to spend thinking about maximizing the investment returns in each client's portfolio? Think about this for a moment.

So, what the financial adviser needs—and what the industry wants to provide—are investment products that are scalable. Investment products that can be rolled out across thousands of clients efficiently. Mutual funds, exchange-traded funds (ETFs), and discretionarily managed portfolios are popular examples. Investment products that are largely "set and forget" and require only occasional tweaking.

These types of investment products generally provide investment performance that is slightly lower than what the overall market delivers, once fees are taken into consideration. To that end, Wall Street is actually good at providing investment solutions to clients who are already wealthy and are focused on preserving what wealth they have.

But Wall Street is very poorly positioned to help those who are not yet wealthy, or those who aspire to grow their wealth quickly. It simply doesn't offer customers the necessary tools to achieve this because those tools aren't scalable or profitable for the industry.

I wrote this book for anyone who wants to beat this system. Anyone who is prepared to educate themselves on how to manage their wealth like a professional trader. If that sounds like you, I'm so glad to have you here!

CHAPTER 2

THE FIVE BIG MYTHS
OF WALL STREET

"Men occasionally stumble over the truth, but most of them pick them-
selves up and hurry off as if nothing had happened."

—WINSTON CHURCHILL

I want to accomplish two things in this chapter:

1. Share with you five of the biggest myths in finance and explain
   why they are holding you back from achieving your financial
   goals
2. Introduce you to the concept of trading psychology

Sections of this chapter may challenge you.

You may have heard some of the myths I am about to share with you
so many times that you have come to believe them—heck, know
them—to be absolute truths. You may have heard them from people
you respect, or regard as experts, which lends them extra gravitas...
but they are still just myths.

For the next few minutes, I ask you to channel your inner curiosity and read with an open mind. As you do so, I'm sure you will agree that all of these myths are completely at odds with common sense.

THE FIVE BIG MYTHS OF FINANCE

"A myth is a fixed way of looking at the world which cannot be destroyed because, looked at through the myth, all evidence supports that myth."

—EDWARD DE BONO

Why do so many of us struggle financially when many of us live in what is arguably the most free and prosperous period in the history of civilization?

Why do we continue to struggle when access to information on how to become wealthy has never been faster, cheaper, and more abundant?

In my view, most of us are kept from our full potential to create wealth because we struggle under false beliefs about money, investing, and finance.

There are hundreds of myths that pervade the finance industry. Maybe I'll share some of the others in another book. But the five myths that follow are the ones that, in my opinion, most commonly hinder aspiring traders from achieving the financial success they desire and deserve.

"It ain't what you don't know that gets you into trouble. It's what you know for sure that just ain't so."

—MARK TWAIN

MYTH NUMBER ONE: 10 PERCENT PER ANNUM IS A FANTASTIC RETURN!

"If we study what is merely average, we will remain merely average."

—SHAWN ACHOR

Here are some examples of very common refrains that are frequently doled out by Wall Street:

- "10 percent is a fantastic return! With interest rates near 0 percent, how could you expect to earn any more on your portfolio?"
- "The market was up 12 percent last year. Your portfolio was up only 10 percent but we took less risk, so all-in-all we have delivered excellent risk-adjusted performance."
- "The S&P 500 fell 10 percent last year but your portfolio only fell in value by 8 percent, so we have outperformed the market and delivered a very sound investment performance."

Do you see anything wrong with this picture?

Perhaps you don't. Quite possibly, these ~~excuses~~ explanations seem perfectly plausible to you.

But the fact is, they are all excuses born out of the impediments of the investment advice industry that we discussed in chapter 1.

Telling you that 10 percent (or any similar figure) per annum is a fantastic return is a function of:

- Wall Street wanting to convince you that this is indeed a great return, so that you won't feel upset when they charge you a heap of fees for delivering what is, in fact, a fairly crappy return.

- The industry not possessing the expertise or resources to deliver a better return (they only want to sell you scalable investment products).
- Wall Street firms don't have the inclination or incentive to deliver strong returns for their clients. Drip-feeding money into a balanced portfolio (aka dollar cost averaging) is much easier than learning the professional risk management techniques and trade setups that you will learn later in this book.
- Everybody else is doing it. Investment advice has become so generic—throw a bunch of money into a diversified portfolio of Exchange Traded Funds (ETFs) and keep drip-feeding money into the portfolio over time. For an investment advice firm to do anything different from what everyone else is doing risks them looking stupid...especially when they lack the proper tools and resources. It's far more comfortable for them to hide in the mediocre majority.

When someone tells you that 10 percent per annum is a great return, they are almost certainly not lying to you intentionally. It's just that they have never been shown how to generate returns of 50 to 100 percent or more on a single trade. I'll show you how this is possible later in this book.

This brings me to my next point: It is NOT your financial adviser's responsibility to ensure your investments perform well. It MUST be YOUR responsibility.

These days it would be more accurate to say that it is your financial adviser's responsibility to ensure you're not a money launderer and that the money you're investing with them is not from the proceeds of crime!

If growing your wealth quickly is important to you, you must make the decision to take responsibility for the performance of your investments. It is too big of a responsibility to outsource to somebody else. And by the time you finish this book, you will be much better equipped than most professionals to undertake this responsibility. Good or *good*?

The fact is, brokers are financially incentivized to get you to trade. This is why brokers will often suggest things to their clients like "switching" from one bank stock to another and then back again. Will selling Citigroup stock in order to switch into Bank of America stock really improve your investment performance? Maybe. Will executing those two transactions help your broker to achieve the monthly revenue targets his boss has set for him? Definitely!

Wealth advisers are financially incentivized to attract more clients, manage more assets under management, and charge high fees on a slew of various investment products.

Very few people in the financial advice industry get paid more if their clients' portfolios perform better or if their clients make more money.

The industry is incentivized to raise assets, sell financial products, or to get you to trade...NOT to make you money!

So, am I saying that you can't trust your financial adviser?

No. Let me be clear, I'm not saying that at all.

But what I am saying is that Wall Street simply doesn't have the resources or the inclination to help individual investors growth their wealth quickly.

Most financial advisers in my experience are smart, honest, hardworking men and women. I would also say that most of them are well-intentioned and have their client's best interests at heart. It's just that the industry doesn't provide them with the tools, or the resources required to help large numbers of clients growth their wealth quickly. Nor are they incentivized by their employers to do so.

If you are already rich, Wall Street firms can do a decent job of keeping you rich. But if you are looking to grow your wealth quickly, you must take on this responsibility yourself. You must acquire the skillset required to generate fantastic returns while managing risk. There will be some learning and some effort involved, but that's what this book is for. Let's do this together.

This is an important skillset that you must seek proactively. It is not taught in schools or universities. Very few parents can teach these skills to their kids. This is the skillset you are starting to learn right now by reading this very book. Well done, I'm proud of you!

MYTH NUMBER TWO: FINANCE IS COMPLEX AND INVESTING IS HARD

"Everything should be made as simple as possible, but not simpler."

—ALBERT EINSTEIN

"Complexity is the enemy of execution."

—ANTHONY ROBBINS

I worked for major global investment banks for the better part of twenty years. Every year, on or about January 3, the office chatter would invariably move from who got drunk and threw up at the office Christmas party to the investment outlook for the new calendar year.

And every year, without fail, the investment outlook that clients would read from investment firms across the world would offer tepid conclusions along the lines of:

- We are therefore cautiously optimistic about the medium-term outlook for the stock market.
- We expect there will be some good opportunities in equities throughout year, however we forecast a rise in volatility.
- We are forecasting value stocks will outperform growth stocks and developed markets will outperform emerging markets. Please contact your investment adviser for a review of your portfolio.

Honestly, if I hear the phrase *cautiously optimistic* ever again, I think I will throw up!

Investment houses are nearly always *cautiously optimistic*. But what does this even mean?

Well, Wall Street wants to keep the investing general public fearful but hopeful.

Fearful enough that you will think you *need* to pay an expert to look after your investment capital (there's that word again).

But hopeful enough of the potential for good investment opportunities, that you will give them your money to look after in the first place.

Wall Street wants you to believe that money *can* be made in investment markets. But also that investment markets are *very difficult* to navigate so you *must* pay an expert to help you.

They want you to believe that yes, it is POSSIBLE to make money in the markets but that you NEED them to help steer you through the troubled waters that are the investment markets.

Wall Street has concocted a complex jargon of financial terms. This is deliberate and it has been done to:

1. Make investing sound more difficult than it really is.
2. Make investment professionals sound more well-informed and intelligent.
3. Make industry outsiders (the general public) feel like they are at a disadvantage.

There will be some jargon in this book (it has become unavoidable I'm afraid). But I will keep it to a minimum and use stories and anecdotes to make it as relatable as possible.

The fact is finance *can be* made to be damn complex and difficult. But it absolutely doesn't need to be in order to make money from the markets.

When it comes to trading, **simpler is almost always better**. Adding layers of complexity only serves to increase uncertainty. And increased uncertainty leads to doubt, doubt leads to fear, and fear is the place where all of your worst nightmares can thrive. Throughout this book we are going to banish unnecessary complexity and fear.

MYTH NUMBER THREE—INVESTING IS SENSIBLE, TRADING IS LIKE GAMBLING

"Wide diversification is only required when investors do not understand what they are doing."

—WARREN BUFFETT

Over the course of my career I have met literally thousands of people who participate in the stock market. If asked, the clear majority of them—I estimate at least 90 percent—would characterize themselves as investors in the market.

It's almost as if there is something less dignified about being a trader. Some people even associate trading stocks with gambling... another prominent myth of finance.

Trader versus Investor

Most people think the difference between an investor and a trader is a function of time.

Supposedly investors have long-term time frames, while traders operate in the short term.

In reality, the difference between the two is a function of purpose, NOT a function of time frame.

Real investors are owners of a business. They buy stock in a company because they understand the business, they believe they're buying in at a fair price, they look forward to participating in the profits of the company over many years, and intend on holding the shares for a long time, often indefinitely.

Everybody else is a trader.

Real traders understand that trends in markets form and persist because of strong, human emotions. They buy and sell stocks because fear and greed create opportunities to profit from the identifiable patterns that form within these trends.

In other words, traders buy a stock (or any other financial asset) because they expect to be able to sell it in the future, at a higher price.

If that sounds anything like you, well my friend you are a trader just like me. This notion may jar you, because you have inherited a perception that traders are short-term focused or like gamblers. These perceptions have been perpetuated by the ill informed (and by people with financial products to sell).

It's an important distinction because most people like to think of themselves as investors—which is probably why so many people have a tough time navigating the stock market successfully.

The fact is that most people are traders, and they get into trouble when they fail to recognize this.

If you've ever bought or sold a stock based on emotion (e.g., "it just felt right" or "I just like Nike products"), you're a trader.

If you check the value of your holdings every day or every week, you're a trader.

If you're pondering how this quarter's earnings will affect a stock's price, you're a trader.

If you wonder how markets will react to the next Federal Open Market Committee (FOMC) statement or next month's employment number, you're a trader.

If you think you should sell Bank of America and buy Citi "because it's cheaper," you're a trader.

We all like to think that we can make rational, logical decisions unaffected by emotion. These are the characteristics of a great investor—but they apply to very few of us.

Indeed, conventional financial theory suggests that investors are rational and seek to maximize profit through objective, nonemotional investment decisions. That makes sense. Nobody invests with the goal of losing money.

However, the powerful emotions of fear and greed (and "FOMO"— the fear of missing out!) along with herd instinct, have always been the main drivers of stock prices and investor behavior. These powerful emotions lead people to make irrational investment decisions. This very fact has given rapid rise to the field of behavioral finance. (For an excellent primer on behavioral finance, I recommend *Misbehaving: The Making of Behavioral Economics* by Richard Thaler.)

Many people who think they're good investors will buy into a stock based on logic and sound reasoning. However, after they've bought in, they will often succumb to the emotions of fear and regret and end up selling winners and hanging onto losers.

There is an old cliché that investors like to toss around that goes: "*You never make a loss until you sell.*" It is often offered as a nugget of wisdom. Really, this cliché has more to do with the ego's reluctance to face up to the regret of loss. I also suspect it's been responsible for the ruination of more traders' accounts than any other Wall Street saying.

"As long as I keep holding this position, it's not really a loss."

—A TRADER WHOSE ACCOUNT WAS
ANNIHILATED A FEW WEEKS LATER

Not knowing what to do with a losing position is the path to disaster for any investor or trader. Most traders (investors) fare poorly in the stock market because they do not have a set plan in place for when the unexpected happens.

Here is a thought experiment I have conducted with hundreds of investors over the years.

Me: "What would you do if the stock you just bought fell 10 percent in price?"

Investor: [Pauses] "Hmm. That's easy. I'd buy more and average in."

Me: "OK, what if it then went on to fall another 10 percent?"

Investor: [Longer pause] "Hmm. I'd buy even more and lower my average cost even more."

Me: "OK, then what if it fell another 10 percent, so now it is down 30 percent from your entry price?"

Investor: [Even longer pause] "Hmmm. I'd buy more because now I'd be getting a bargain!"

Me: "OK, so what if it now fell another 10 percent, so it was down 40 percent from your entry price?"

Investor: [Long pause, looks slightly perplexed and even mildly panicked] "Well, if it fell 40 percent, I'd sell everything and cut my losses. I'm not stupid!"

So, if the stock falls 30 percent you're still buying more, but if it falls 40 percent, you'll sell everything?

Does this sound like a well-reasoned plan to you?

The fact is most investors have no idea what to do when something unexpected happens because they are completely unprepared for the unexpected.

It's crucial to accept and appreciate that anything can (and does!) happen in markets and to prepare accordingly. This is what so few investors are taught to do. "Buy and hold" and they are told, "Invest for the long term," but this tepid advice does nothing to help the investor who, during a bear market, is in the grip of fear as markets fall day after day.

You are probably familiar with the famous Mike Tyson quote: *"Everybody has a plan until they get punched in the mouth."* Well, unexpected events in the stock market are the metaphorical "punch in the mouth" for investors. Risk management teaches us what to do while getting punched and it is the foundation to your success as a trader. We will cover risk management in detail in chapter 12.

The unfortunate fact is investors often don't fare much better even when things are going their way. They will get into a solid gain on a position but will refuse to take profits...even if it has met their wildest expectations. Often, they will find new reasons to hold on as greed—or fear of missing out (FOMO)—has taken over and they don't want to leave potential gains on the table. Our ego also loves to see that it has been clever enough to have bought a stock that now has a nice, unrealized profit. The ego feels a flush of pride whenever it sees a profitable position in your brokerage account.

Often, after seeing a nice gain, the stock will fall back down towards the purchase price, leaving the investor without a plan and completely unsure about what to do next. You can see the potential negative effects that fear and greed can have on the average investor's returns, if they are not aware of and in control of these emotions.

Whether they admit it or not, most participants in the stock market are traders. A good trader knows that when it comes to markets, emotion will (nearly) always override logic. She can spot emotional extremes in the market and knows how to exploit them for profit. More importantly, she is aware of her own emotions and has rules in place to keep them in check.

To be a profitable trader, you must follow a robust set of trading rules and develop strong risk management discipline; you must apply them with consistency. This will take emotions out of the equation as much as possible and keep you on the right side of the market.

Why Trading Is NOT Gambling

I was chatting with a mate of mine over a cup of kopi (local coffee) one morning in Singapore. We were talking about the markets and stock trading. This friend is financially literate, but he doesn't work in the investment industry. He was asking me about what stocks I'd been trading, so I gave him a rundown on what I'd been making money on and what I'd lost some money on.

I then asked him what he was doing with his trading these days. He told me he had vowed against trading stocks after his experience in 2008 when he lost a bundle of money. No more gambling for him! He was sticking to only buying and holding ETFs and "blue chip" stocks from now on. He saw himself as an investor these days!

This is a point of view that I've never really agreed with.

When someone buys an ETF or index fund, they are not a long-term investor in a company whose cash flows they have modeled and whose valuation they understand. They are buying a financial asset with the expectation that they'll be able to sell it at a higher price at some point in the future.

Buying index funds and ETFs therefore fits the very definition of trading.

Now consider that just about every smart financial commentator in the world today is spouting the virtues of ETFs and index funds to anybody who will listen to them. All the while, nobody is recommending that people devote 40 percent of their net worth to playing blackjack. How come? Ah...because blackjack is gambling! So then why is it OK to put 40 percent of our assets into ETFs? Because, apparently, buying ETFs is *not* gambling.

So, my mate as well as many professionals in the financial advice industry say trading is gambling. But billionaire hedge fund managers like Paul Tudor Jones and David Tepper say trading is not gambling.

Who is right?

To answer that, we need to understand motivation, intent, and odds.

Motivation, Intent, and Odds

Let us now explore the psychology of a gambler and compare it with the psychology of a successful trader. We'll start by asking: what are gamblers looking for? What is their motivation?

Gamblers are looking for an outsized, lottery-style payoff and something they have not worked for. Something they know that they will be lucky to get.

If I put $100 on red at the roulette table, I know I don't deserve to win. Over time, my odds of winning one spin after a bet of red or black are just 47.37 percent. Of course, I might win that one time, but deep down I know I can't win over the long term. If I'm playing the long game, it is statistically probable that I'm going to lose money.

And therein lies the thrill of it! If I put $100 on red and win, I've done something a little bit naughty, something I know I shouldn't do, but I've gotten away with it!

If I get away with it, I've successfully beaten odds that were mathematically against me and come out the other side smiling. A bit like surviving a wipeout on a monster wave, or riding a roller coaster, it's a rush, and many people love that rush.

There's nothing thrilling about buying an index fund—or any other "safe" "investment." We know that over a long enough time frame we have a good chance to win. Nothing naughty or exciting about that. Putting money in a term deposit or a government bond is a yawn-fest. There's zero chance I'm going to somehow make 100 percent on my money but also a (near) zero chance I'm going to lose money either. I'm highly likely to make 2 percent on my money and that's it.

But trading is not passively buying an ETF. And it's certainly not a term deposit. There are no guarantees in trading. So, does that make trading, gambling?

Well to be honest, it depends.

When Buying Shares *Is* like Gambling

If I pick a random penny stock to buy, this is gambling, and I'll explain why.

Again, it's all about the odds and the intent. The only reason I'm buying a penny stock is my belief/hope that I will make a lottery-like return on it. But the odds of my penny stock achieving a 10x return are unknowable. It might? But it probably won't. Yet, my intent is to make out big by getting lucky.

When the odds are unknowable or when I'm wishing for incredible luck—THAT is gambling!

How about picking a "blue chip" stock? If it's a random pick, it's not so different. It's less likely to drop to zero dollars, but the odds are still unknowable, as is the expected payoff.

What if it's not a random pick, but rather a careful selection based on research? The first question we need to ask is: what are the odds? Looking at the fundamentals, we could ask a question like "how many stocks have had similar fundamentals of the stock we like, and then went on to achieve 'x' percent gain within a time frame of 'y'?" If we can't answer this, we're still gambling because really, we're still hoping to get lucky.

If we do know the answer, then we're making an informed decision. Some might call it an investment decision. We know our odds and profit target, when to cut our losses if it's going badly, and when to take our profits if the fundamentals change.

So, What about Trading?

The first thing a good trader asks herself before she places a trade is "what's the risk on this trade, and is the potential reward worth the potential risk?" Once she has found a high probability trade setup she likes, the first thing she needs to define is her stop-loss. This is her line in the sand. The point at which she is 'happy enough' to be proven wrong, take a small loss on the trade, and flow to a new opportunity. Then, she needs to assess her profit targets. Factors like support and resistance, volatility, and momentum all play a part in determining where she is likely to take her profit.

If she's risking 8 percent on a trade that looks like it may only make 4 percent before stalling...well, she probably doesn't want to be placing trades (bets!) like those on a regular basis.

The other question a trader needs to keep asking is "what can I expect my trading system to do for me over the long term?"

We want to know, when using a trading method, that our profits over time will exceed our losses (yes, there will be losses!).

Trading Expectancy

The profitability of a trading method over time is determined by *expectancy*.

Expectancy is calculated as follows:

> Expectancy = (Probability of a Win * Average Win) − (Probability of a Loss * Average Loss)

For example, assume a trading method produces profitable trades 60 percent of the time and losing trades 40 percent of the time. The average winning trade gains 10 percent while losing trades on average lose 5 percent. For a $10,000 account the expectancy for this trading method will be:

$$(60\% * \$1,000) - (40\% * \$500) = \$400$$

This means, on average, over time (over hundreds of trades) each trade will contribute $400 to the overall profit and loss on the trader's account. Which is fantastic!

A Trader's Mindset

People don't go to their regular day jobs hoping that today is the day it will be announced that they've won $1 million from their employer. They go knowing that the odds of their job producing a certain amount of income are high, and their goal is to accumulate that income over time.

Successful trading is the same way.

Unfortunately, many traders approach the trading profession with a "lotto-ticket" mindset. "I'll be happy if I can turn my $2,000 into $1,000,000 within a year." This sort of mindset will almost guarantee your failure as a trader. You will trade too big, take too much risk, and place far too much pressure on yourself, in an attempt to reach such lofty goals.

A healthy trading mindset is when you:

- Treat trading as a profession
- Are putting a specific skillset to use in order to generate income and/or account growth

Much like a real job, really.

MYTH NUMBER FOUR: "BUY AND HOLD" IS THE ONLY RATIONAL INVESTMENT STRATEGY

"Never accept conventional wisdom in finance. If others keep failing, why do you want to follow them?"

—ZIAD ABDELNOUR

This myth may challenge you a little more, as it is so deeply entrenched in the psyche of most people.

"Buy and hold" is the foundation—the absolute bedrock—of the investment advice industry. Almost everyone who derives their income for delivering investment advice is singing the praises of "buy and hold" from the rooftops. This is because, as we saw in chapter 1, buy and hold style investment products are highly scalable.

It is a widely held belief in our society that wealth is determined by how much money we have saved in the bank, our investment portfolio, or in retirement accounts, regardless of any other factor. This myth dominates our thoughts and conversations on personal finance, and we accept it without question.

According to mainstream financial media, the road to wealth is to save your ass off and accumulate as much money as you can from your salary, with the pie-in-the-sky dream of living off the interest we earn on all the money we've managed to save.

We're taught to cut our expenses at all costs, squirrel money away in a 401(k) or IRA or superannuation fund, find out what our "risk tolerance" is, and determine the appropriate asset allocation.

"Skipping lattes won't make you wealthy."

—T. HARV EKER

Risk Tolerance and Asset Allocation

"Risk tolerance" is defined as the degree of uncertainty that an investor can handle regarding a negative change in the value of his or her portfolio.

Financial institutions will often have you complete a questionnaire asking how you feel about risk to determine your "risk profile" and then your asset allocation.

Until you have lived through a bear market and seen equity markets get cut in half in real time, you have no idea what your risk tolerance really is. Answering lame questions about how you would hypothetically feel if the value of your hypothetical portfolio dropped a hypothetical 30 percent has zero relevance unless you've lived through such an experience.

"Asset allocation" is a strategy that promises to reduce risk by dividing an investment portfolio among different categories such as stocks, bonds, real estate, private equity, and cash. Traditional asset allocation (also known as diversification) sounds great in theory, but it will fail you when you most need it...i.e., when the shit is hitting the fan!

Diversification aims to exploit the theory of investing in different asset classes (e.g., stocks, bonds, and property) that have a low correlation with each other. That is, asset classes that will rise and fall at different times, and move in different cycles, with the aim of smoothing out fluctuations in the value of your portfolio. The big problem is that when a crisis hits, these different asset classes start to correlate with each other very closely. When fear strikes the markets, all asset classes tend to fall at the same time.

DALBAR's 2016 Quantitative Analysis of Investor Behavior (QAIB) had this to say on diversification:

> Asset classes tend to become more correlated during market corrections, somewhat muting the benefits of diversification and necessitating a downside protection strategy that goes beyond traditional diversification.

In other words, diversification works fine when you really don't need it (when markets are relaxed and trending up) and fails you terribly when you need it most (when financial markets are going to hell in a handbasket).

When the next recessionary bear market comes (when, not if), not having a hedging strategy or at least a risk management discipline in place is going to expose investors to significant capital destruction.

The Only Way Is Up!

The other problem with the conventional buy and hold (buy and hope) method of investing is that you can only make money when markets rise.

If the stock market corrects, enters a bear market, or crashes, you are going to lose money. You are going to feel stressed and miserable, and be prone to making lower quality decisions as a result. And no, traditional diversification won't save you.

It is true that markets rise over time. The stock market rises about 75 percent of the time, in fact. But stock market falls tend to happen so quickly, and the falls can be so significant and so deleterious to the value of your wealth, that not learning how to make money during a falling market means leaving a LOT of money on the table. I will go as far as to say it is irresponsible not to learn how to make money in falling markets, if you're going to put your money to work in the markets at all. Stock markets really do climb up the stairs and fall down the elevator shaft.

Financial institutions will not teach you how to profit from a falling market because they do not have the necessary tools or expertise. That is why they are always telling you to "focus on the long term."

Having the ability to make money in rising AND falling markets means you can approach the market without emotion. You're not constantly rooting for the market to rise and feeling fear (or nausea!) when the market falls. You can watch market action with genuine curiosity, rather than feeling waves of euphoria and fear. This is a very powerful way to approach the markets and it's the approach I am going to teach you in this book.

The Accumulation Theory

Financial pundits teach us to "invest" in mutual funds or "discretionary portfolios," and to sacrifice our current desires and potential to achieve some imagined, far-off goal. This theory teaches us to accumulate as much money as possible and let it sit stagnant in a 401(k) or superannuation fund for years (if not decades), increasing at a glacial pace, if at all.

Maybe you've heard about the supposed wonders of compound interest?

Maybe you've even heard how compound interest is the "eighth wonder of the world?"

Look, compound interest is great when interest rates are double-digit AND you already have a lot of money. But when rates are in the 0 to 2 percent range...save hard, compound your interest, and you might be able to double your money *every five generations*.

Does this sound exciting to you? No, of course it doesn't. That's because compound interest sucks in today's environment unless you are happy with glacially slow growth on your money.

Here are some facts about why these theories of "buy and hold" investing are propagated by Wall Street:

1. Financial institutions want your money to manage.
2. They want it on a regular, systematic basis (preferably through automatic contribution).
3. They will charge you fees for managing your money, whether you make money or not.

4. Once they have your money, they will try their damnedest to hold onto it for as long as possible (which is why early withdrawal restrictions, early termination fees, and lockup periods exist).

The magic pill that the entire financial advice industry is built on— and that most of us have swallowed—is that financial success comes from investing in the right products, employing the right strategies, and making a heap of assumptions based on hundreds or thousands of unknowable variables.

This, despite the fact that it's working for hardly anyone. I'll let the dismal statistics speak for themselves.

A Gallup survey conducted in May 2017 showed that 75 percent of workers in the US want to retire before age 60, yet only 25 percent think they will be able to.

According to a study conducted by the US Department of Commerce, only 5 percent of all Americans are financially independent by age 65. Fully 75 percent of retirees are forced to depend on family, friends, and social security for sources of income, and 51 percent of retirees today have incomes below $10,000 per year.

In a world filled with financial advice, very few have enjoyed financial success. Conventional wisdom when it comes to investing and growing wealth is not working for the majority of us.

I believe one of the biggest traps humans fall into is sacrificing the present moment for some imagined, intangible, and unpredictable future. This behavior encourages a scarcity mindset.

We are constantly sacrificing today for tomorrow.

We are working our asses off and saving our asses off today, all for tomorrow.

But tomorrow never comes.

We only ever live our lives right now. We will never live our life tomorrow. Yesterday is a dream. Tomorrow is an illusion. So, we should do what we can to make right now awesome.

The finance industry is full of pundits like Suze Orman who dish out horrible advice like: if you waste your money on coffee, "you are peeing $1 million down the drain as you are drinking that coffee." This sort of advice just perpetuates the scarcity mindset.

Here's the big wake-up call folks: YOU CAN'T SAVE YOUR WAY TO PROSPERITY!

In order to achieve prosperity, you need to approach life with a growth mindset rather than a scarcity mindset. This means you need to find ways of generating additional sources of income, rather than skipping coffees and clipping coupons.

The conventional way of thinking about money is to think of it like a smartphone battery.

Every month, as we pay for rent, groceries, car payments, and insurance, the battery gets depleted. Then our paycheck comes in and the battery is recharged. We go through this endless cycle of depletion and recharging but rarely do we explore solutions, such as, "how do I upgrade to a bigger battery?" or "why don't I just get a second battery?"

The great news is that trading is the quickest, easiest way I have discovered to generate a second income (get a second battery!). Trading requires minimal capital outlay, it can be learned relatively quickly, it can be done part time, and you don't need to hire any staff!

With trading, you are constantly learning; it definitely never gets boring!

It is much easier, much less stressful—and if done properly, much lower risk—than buying a franchise or setting up your own business.

And the other great thing about trading? It is a skill and a career you can pursue for the rest of your life, well into retirement. With experience, it may only take you twenty minutes per day to generate that second income. Meaning you could end up with both the time and the financial resources to pursue the life of your dreams.

MYTH NUMBER FIVE: HIGH RISK = HIGH RETURNS

"Higher risk should equal higher average return. But when it comes to volatility, low risk equals high return. You get paid more not to take risk! That flies in the face of everything finance theorists believe."

—NOAH SMITH

When you meet with a financial planner, one of the first things he will ask you to do is complete one of those asinine risk profile questionnaires we talked about earlier in this chapter. He will ask questions about how long you think it will be before you need to access the money, what you would do if the market fell, how well can you tolerate volatility, etc.

The planner needs to know how much risk you can handle, because according to conventional finance theory, the higher the risk you can handle, the greater the returns you can get. In fact, it has been completely drilled into us that we can only dream of getting high returns if we're willing to subject ourselves to significant amounts of risk.

But what is risk, exactly?

Risk is the possibility of loss. The possibility of a permanent loss of your capital.

So what the finance industry is telling us is that in order to increase our chances of winning, we must increase our chances of losing. And the investing public has been buying this nonsense for decades! But ask yourself, how does this make any logical sense whatsoever?

The theory that high returns necessitate high risk comes from people selling cookie-cutter investment products. It comes from the unsound notion that "investing" means throwing money mindlessly into a 401(k), superannuation fund, mutual fund, or to "buy shares for the long term" in companies we know little about and have no hope of influencing. After which, we hope we get lucky and make some money.

Let me propose an alternate theory and ask you how it measures up:

To increase our returns, we must take responsibility for increasing our chances of winning and decreasing our chances of losing.

Sounds logical, right? And yet, this is NOT what we are being taught!

I think it is more logical and more instructive to equate returns with effort, rather than risk.

If you want to exert zero effort, and mindlessly dump your money with a money manager or into a financial product, you cannot expect much return (and you really have NO IDEA what your risk is, or what you should do if something unexpected happens).

If you are one of the rare individuals who is prepared to acquire the knowledge, and then complete the ongoing work of finding high probability trade setups while properly managing your risk, you can enjoy *exceptional* returns. The types of returns people without this knowledge would dismiss as impossible. We will get to that later in this book, I promise!

Using the information detailed in the following pages, I have taught novice traders who have gone on to double or triple their trading accounts in a matter of weeks. They are achieving the types of returns on their money that are completely out of reach to those following conventional wisdom.

Many on Wall Street say things like "it's impossible to beat the market," or "it's impossible to make a living from trading." There are plenty of haters out there. One thing I can guarantee you—the haters who are saying such things have never been successful traders in their own right, so why listen to them?

Remember too, that Wall Street doesn't want individuals like you to become successful at trading, because you'd cease paying them fees.

But saying something like "it's impossible to make a living from trading" is literally the equivalent of saying "it's impossible to fly a Boeing 787." It seems impossible to those who haven't acquired the necessary skillset. Helping you to acquire the necessary skillset is what I'm here for; together we can do this.

CHAPTER 3

WHY TRADING IS LIKE SEX

There are many reasons why trading is like sex:

- We talk about "naked positions" all the time.
- Trading can sound kinda kinky when we talk about straddles and strangles.
- With both trading and sex, you have to participate to enjoy the benefits. They can both get a little rough at times, but they always end with an ahh.

"A bull market is like sex because it feels best just before it ends."

—BARTON BIGGS

Now get that smirk off your face...this is a serious chapter! I will reveal the REAL reason why trading is like sex a little later.

This chapter is on trading psychology. However, I realized that if I called this chapter "trading psychology" you might skip it. I briefly introduced the concept of trading psychology in chapter 2, when contrasting the mindset of a trader with that of a gambler. This chapter will be more of a deep dive on this crucial subject. Don't worry, it's going to be fun!

By the end of this chapter, you will have learned some valuable insights into how to develop a winning trader's mindset. The development of this mindset is not just important. It's necessary for your success. The markets are like a mirror. They will reflect back to you whatever deep-seated attitudes you may have about money, success, your sense of self-worth, and what you believe you deserve.

At the core of developing a winning trader's mindset is ensuring the emotional brain is never allowed to run the show. You want to ensure your logical, unemotional, executive brain is always in control when trading.

I've been doing this for a long time, and I can nearly always tell whereabouts somebody is on their trading journey simply by the types of questions they ask.

New traders will ask "what indicators do you use?" or "what types of moving averages should I put on my chart?" This is akin to the novice golfer wondering what sort of golf clubs they should buy. Unfortunately, many traders (and golfers!) never progress beyond obsessing over what shiny new equipment they should buy to improve their game. They mistakenly hope that a new driver—rather than hours spent at the driving range—is what will help them advance.

"I should buy a new lob wedge to improve my short game!" equates to "I should tweak the settings on my MACD indicator to improve my trading!"

Working on yourself and improving your mindset is going to be vastly more rewarding to you in any endeavor you choose to undertake, trading included. However, this is a fact that very few people want to hear. These days everybody is looking for a shortcut or "life hack."

Anyway, back to the questions traders ask along their trading journey.

A trader with a little more experience will ask "how do I know when to get into a trade?" or "where should I set my stop-loss?" This is like the inexperienced golfer working on their stance and their grip, and hopefully starting to hit some balls off the driving range.

An intermediate trader will ask "what should my position sizing strategy look like?" and "what risk management rules should I follow?" Now the golfer has played a few rounds of golf and wants to know how to shape their shots and get their score down.

An advanced trader invariably wants to talk about psychology and mindset. They will ask "how do I stop my emotional brain from damaging my game?" or "how many times have you read Mark Douglas's *Trading in the Zone?*" Similarly, the advanced golfer who has grooved a good swing has the epiphany that at a certain point, golf is 90 percent a mental game, just like trading.

If new traders could approach trading with a winning mindset to begin with, it would literally save them years of frustration, heartache, losing trades, and missed opportunities. Most traders either quit or blow up their trading account before ever obtaining a good trading mindset. This is something I want to rectify with this book.

Proper mindset is crucial to your success in trading. It's crucial to your success in most areas of your life, but trading is one area where a sub-optimal mindset will cause you to bleed money in an obvious and frustrating fashion. That's why "trading psychology" is in chapter 3 and not chapter 12 of this book...and also why this chapter has a sexy title—I really need you to read and absorb this information!

Fear not, I have not tried to trick you. Trading really is like sex. So, back to the analogy:

Trading is like sex in that if you can just focus on enjoying (and getting good at) the *process*—without having any specific objectives in mind—the outcomes will be all-the-more rewarding.

I get that the desire to grow our account or generate a regular income from the market is why most of us get into trading in the first place. But this is honestly the last thing you want to focus on... particularly in the early stages of your development as a trader.

It's like the mountain climber who wants to scale the mountain in order to reach the summit. Summiting cannot be the climber's focus during the climb...particularly at the start of the climb. She must focus, step by step, on where to place her hands and feet from one moment to the next. That is, she must focus on the process of climbing. If she does a good job of that, the ultimate objective of summiting safely will be realized.

To drive the sex metaphor all the way to its ~~climax~~ logical conclusion: trading profits are like orgasms—the more you focus on having them, the harder they are to obtain!

Trading becomes easy once a trader learns to ignore her own personal opinions, stops trying to be right, stops focusing on making money, and instead focuses on the process of trading.

"The goal of a successful trader is to make the best trades. Money is secondary."

—ALEXANDER ELDER

WHY LEARNING TO TRADE IS DIFFERENT FROM LEARNING TO FLY A PLANE

One of the frequent problems I see with many novice traders is their expectation that they will be wildly successful within a very short period of time and with minimal training. This is like somebody expecting to be able to jump into the flight deck of a Boeing 787, take off, fly across the Atlantic, and land it successfully without any prior training. I think you'll agree this seems insane.

Yet traders will routinely open a trading account and start trading with little-to-no training...and be surprised when they're not successful. This is equally insane. There is a reason why this profession is called "trading" and not "guaranteed profits."

Now, with all due respect to airline pilots (my dad flew for British Airways for over thirty years, so aircraft analogies come naturally to me), learning to trade might be even more difficult than learning to fly an aircraft.

You see, if you want to learn to fly a plane, the aircraft manufacturer will supply you with all of the manuals, documentation, and support necessary for your education. In other words, there is a known source of truth that you can trust. This source will deliver all the correct information you need to be successful in learning to fly the plane.

With trading—there is no such single source of truth. In fact, there are literally thousands of books, thousands of courses, millions of different trading methods...and many of them are crap! Peddled by people who have never worked in the trenches or been successful traders in their own right.

A proper trading education is essential, but this education must go beyond technical indicators, setups, and risk management. Yes, those things are all important, but a trader aspiring for success must also learn about psychology and emotional control. And that is exactly what we are covering in this chapter.

I've taught winning setups to many traders, but the ones who don't "get" or won't incorporate the psychology part always end up losing money eventually. What is so deceptive about this process is that having the wrong mindset doesn't mean every trade is a loser. Far from it. But all it takes is one nasty downward psychological spiral to turn a successful trader into one who screws everything up.

When trading the markets, there exists the potential for you to make a fortune or lose everything. Skill matters. For the one willing to learn and conscientiously apply what they have learned in a disciplined manner, this is wonderful news! For the part-time amateur, it's a recipe for an expensive education. Tourists don't fare well in the financial markets.

A properly educated trader will create an income stream for life, from a specific set of skills. A poorly educated trader will literally enable their own financial self-destruction.

DO YOU WANT TO BE RIGHT, OR DO YOU WANT TO MAKE MONEY?

Do you know what your job as a trader is?

What if I told you your job is NOT to be right?

It's NOT to predict what's going to happen in the future.

It's NOT to pick tops and bottoms in the market.

It's NOT staring at charts all day.

It's NOT listening to mainstream media in order to stay up to date with the "news."

No, your job is much simpler than all of that.

Your ONLY job as a trader is to manage the net liquidating value (NLV) of your trading account, such that it rises over time. That's it! (NLV is the cash value of your account if all of your positions were closed at market.)

Do you want to be right or do you want to make money? It honestly took me years to really understand and appreciate what this saying means (I believe it is attributed to Ned Davis of Ned Davis Research). The need to be "right" is what ties so many aspiring traders up in knots. The goal of trading is to be consistently profitable, not consistently right. Yes, there is a difference.

A trader's job is not to be right. Her job is, in fact, to take lots of SMALL losses. Here is where our human brain is hard wired to work against us when it comes to trading.

You see, from the time you were two years old, you've been trying your best not to screw anything up, not to make mistakes, not to get anything wrong. Growing up, if you did something wrong, your parents would scold you—maybe even punish you. Your teachers would tell you off, your friends would make fun of you, and your boss would yell at you. As a result, you've grown up believing that being wrong or making a mistake is inherently bad, and something to be avoided at all costs. You've grown up learning to "not make mistakes." Or worse, you're attempting to hide, lie about, ignore, or shift the blame for your mistakes. This lifelong mindset has been subconsciously driving your decisions, and it will drive the trading decisions of improperly educated traders.

"Mistakes are always forgivable, if one has the courage to admit them."
—BRUCE LEE

Here's an example of how this can work. Because we're naturally fearful of making mistakes in trading (also known as losing money), we're scared of pulling the trigger on good setups. We wait until the pain of not being involved in the very move that we predicted becomes so great, that we chase the trade and jump in (also known as fear of missing out, or FOMO). Or maybe you enter a trade and straight away it moves against you. You feel a sense of disappointment—or maybe even shame—at having made a poor entry, which your ego interprets as a mistake. You feel reluctant to open your brokerage account and have this losing trade stare you in the face, because every time you do those feelings of shame resurface. Before you know it, what started as a small, manageable loss has turned into a significant loss that makes you feel sick every time you think about it.

If you're not aware of these subconscious machinations, you will be a slave to your emotions and the market will have its wicked way with you.

You'll do almost anything to avoid being wrong or making a mistake. And if you do make a mistake, you may have trouble owning up to it. You may ignore it or blame somebody else (or even "the market") for it.

This mindset will get you killed in trading. You will become the market's bitch.

Here's a fact: in trading, losses are inevitable.

In trading, we only deal with probabilities, never certainties. Failure to realize and accept this can lead us to:

1. Feel stupid or shameful for making a trading loss.
2. Treat trading losses as personal—"the market is out to get me!"

As professional traders, we will have losing trades! Our responsibility is to mercilessly cut them off at the knees before they have the opportunity to destroy our trading account. There is no shame in taking a small loss. In fact, having the courage to admit you're wrong on a trade, and taking action to prevent a small loss from becoming a big loss should be considered a victory!

We are taught from a young age to think in a deterministic manner. To think in terms of cause and effect: if A happens, then B will happen. However, every trade we place is probabilistic in nature. If A happens, then B is more likely to happen, but anything CAN happen.

Even adhering to the best trading system, we will encounter losses. Realize that we are always dealing with probabilities, never certainties. Trading losses are not mistakes. They are simply one of a trader's operating expenses. They are an inevitable cost of doing business. They are also part of the cost of education for new traders.

"What is defeat? Nothing but education; nothing but the first step to something better."

—WENDELL PHILLIPS

Understand that so long as you have followed your trading plan, you have not made a mistake, regardless of the eventual outcome of the trade.

However, like any profitable business, we naturally want to keep our expenses to a minimum. This is why it is essential to trade with an edge.

So, what's an edge?

An edge is "something" that stacks the probabilities in our favor. And that "something" is a trading method that:

- Highlights high probability entries for us
- Guides us when to take profit
- Informs us how to manage risk

These are the key mechanical elements of trading that I will teach you in the remaining chapters of this book.

The following are my key pieces of advice on developing a winning trader's mindset.

EMOTIONAL CONTROL

"The key to trading success is emotional discipline. If intelligence were the key, there would be a lot more people making money trading."

—VICTOR SPERANDEO

You certainly don't need to be in the top 1 percent of intelligence to make money in the market. You just need to be in the top 49 percent of being able to recognize and control your emotions.

If you are a slave to your emotions, trading is just not going to work. You can read every book on trading ever written, attend a ton of webinars, and still not become a profitable trader. Knowledge is important, but it's not the holy grail of trading. The mind—and emotions—is the final frontier every trader must conquer to realize their full potential. But it is also the part we resist working on the most.

Choose the nonemotional response to ANY life situation, and you will see how much easier your life becomes. This is one area where trading does imitate life. When trading, you must keep your emotional brain from making the decisions at all costs. The executive brain (the pre-frontal cortex) must remain in control.

Think of something you reacted to emotionally a few months ago. Maybe it was a fight with your spouse, an argument with your boss, or maybe you yelled at one of your kids. Thinking back on that event today, you're likely to think "what the hell was I thinking?" The fact is, you weren't thinking. You were reacting. You were on emotional autopilot. But now that the emotional charge of the event has drained away, you can see more clearly because the chemical cocktail of stress hormones has long since left your body.

Markets ebb and flow, and with it, so do our emotions. Failure to recognize this will lead to a trading account where your money also ebbs and flows (or maybe it just flows out!).

In short—emotion is the enemy of successful trading. The markets are literally set up to take advantage of and prey upon human nature.

Markets always try to exact as much pain as possible on as many people as possible, moving sharply only once enough people get trapped on the wrong side of a trade. When that happens, an outpouring of fear, frustration, and rage spills on the markets. The well-prepared trader can spot this release of emotion in price and use his knowledge to enter a high probability trade.

The two most damaging emotions a trader will encounter are fear and euphoria.

If you approach the market fearfully, you start thinking fearfully and you will come up with fearful solutions. Fear causes stress, and stress literally makes you stupid. See yourself as a professional risk manager first and foremost, and there is simply no need for fear.

Approach the markets the same way you would a large dog. If you approach the dog fearfully, thinking "oh I'm scared, I wonder if the dog will bite me," your interaction with the dog is unlikely to be a satisfying experience for either of you. If you approach the dog with a calm attitude of "good dog, I bet you'd love a scratch behind the ear," the odds of a favorable outcome increase dramatically. And so it is with the markets.

Things can get even worse when we're feeling euphoric. After a succession of big wins, our ego tends to swell and we become victims of pride, as we believe we have finally "got markets all figured out." It is at this point we stop being thorough in doing our homework, become blasé about our entries, and lose discipline on exits and risk management, on the newfound belief that we are now God's gift to trading. This lack of focus and discipline inevitably leads to some losing trades...and a sharp lesson in humility delivered by "Mr. Market" himself.

One of the keys to successful emotional control is position sizing. Regardless of your level of trading experience, it is of paramount importance not to trade a position size that freaks you out. If your maximum potential loss on a position is a number that keeps you awake at night, you can bet your emotional brain is running the show, even if you're oblivious to this fact. Cut your position size until you are completely un-freaked out by your maximum potential loss. You never want to feel surges of emotion—positive or negative—with each upswing or downswing in the market.

Now, I'm not saying that I never feel a range of emotions when I'm trading. I am human, after all. I've just become good at stopping the emotions in my head from travelling down to my hand which moves and clicks my mouse.

There are many other "non-trading" techniques I use and recommend, that help us regulate our emotions. They include breathwork, EFT/tapping, and meditation.

BREATHWORK

Breathwork is handy as it can help us in the here-and-now. Three of my preferred breathwork techniques are:

4-7-8 breath—This is a great stress antidote than can put you in a more relaxed state almost immediately. To practice this breath, sit in a chair with your back straight and gently place the tip of your tongue against the roof of your mouth. Make sure your lungs are fully empty. Then inhale through your nose for a count of four. I synchronize my count with my heartbeat as I find this helps to keep me centered, while maintaining a focus on my heart. After filling your lungs with air to a four count, hold your breath for a count of seven (don't worry, it's easier than it sounds!). After holding for seven, exhale through your mouth (and around your tongue!) through pursed lips for a count of eight. You should have expelled all of the air from your lungs after the eight count. Once this is done, repeat the cycle three more times, for a total of four cycles.

What I love about the 4-7-8 breath is that it relaxes you and energizes your brain at the same time. I do four rounds of 4-7-8 breathing before analyzing my trades and before trading live in the market. This helps to reduce any emotional charge I may be feeling. I highly recommend this practice for stress management. Don't overdo it though...four cycles is enough!

4-8 breath—If the 4-7-8 breath isn't for you, you can try the 4-8 breath. This is simply inhaling for a count of four and exhaling for a count of eight. Again, I synchronize my count to my heartbeat. I find the 4-8 breath great for relaxation, but it can make me a little too relaxed (read: sleepy). I find this one great to do at bedtime.

Any breathwork where the exhale is noticeably longer than the inhale activates the parasympathetic nervous system. This is the part of your autonomic nervous system that is responsible for "rest and digest." It deactivates the sympathetic nervous system which controls the body's "fight or flight" response. This results in a calmer, less emotional you.

Box Breathing—Yet another method you can try to reduce stress in the here-and-now is box breathing. In this technique you inhale for a count of four, hold your breath for a four count, exhale to a four count, and then hold for another four count while your lungs are empty.

All of these breathwork techniques are good for lowering your heart rate, activating your parasympathetic nervous system, and helping you to feel calmer and less reactive.

MEDITATION

"Between stimulus and response there is a space. In that space is our

power to choose our response. In our response lies our growth and our freedom."

—VIKTOR FRANKL

Unlike breathwork, which can deliver effective results almost immediately, the benefits of meditation accumulate over time.

The key benefits I have gained from meditation include:

- Being more aware of, and in tune with my emotional state. This is very important for traders.
- Better recognizing the space that exists between an external stimulus and my response. Meditation means I have a greater chance of responding to a situation rather than reacting to it.

There are thousands of different meditation techniques and apps out there. If you like the idea of a guided meditation with an app, I think Sam Harris's Waking Up app is excellent. Not only are the meditations great, but what you learn along the way about meditation is also very useful.

If you prefer the idea of "unplugged" meditation, I recommend Ziva Meditation by Emily Fletcher. I have taken the Ziva online course and found it very empowering. I highly recommend it if you don't want to rely on an app.

EFT/TAPPING

If breathwork helps in the here-and-now and meditation provides amazing benefits over the long term, I think of EFT as the "bridge" between the two. EFT can provide almost immediate relief, but it is also great for deprogramming limiting beliefs and easing emotional trauma over the longer term.

If you would like to learn more about EFT, I recommend you check out Dawson Church's EFT Universe. It's a wonderful resource with a whole host of information to get you started.

As Dawson Church says in his excellent book, *Mind to Matter*:

> The parts of the brain tasked with emotional regulation are also the ones that handle working memory...Working memory involves awareness, enabling you to remain focused on an activity and to sort relevant from irrelevant information. When your emotions are disturbed, those parts of the brain go offline for use by working memory. You then make poor decisions. When you learn effective emotional regulation, you are able to control your emotions, freeing up the brain's memory circuits to run your life wisely.

CONSISTENCY IS KEY

"What you do every day matters more than what you do once in a while."

—GRETCHEN RUBIN

Anybody can make money on the next trade. Anybody. Don't believe me? Well think of it like this.

Anybody can throw a basketball through the hoop on the next shot. Anybody. But how many times can they get the ball through the hoop on the next 1,000 shots?

Being profitable over the course of hundreds and thousands of trades is what counts, and this is statistically HIGHLY IMPROBA-BLE without a disciplined trading plan.

If as a trader you can master consistency, the world becomes your oyster. These are some of the things that become possible for you when you commit to consistency in your trading:

- Generate a regular income stream from the market
- Limit your drawdowns and therefore your risk
- Develop confidence and belief in yourself as a trader
- Grow your equity
- Not blow up your account
- Spend lots more time on stuff you like doing

Consistency is maximizing the number of times you can shoot the ball through the hoop on the next 1,000 shots. Consistency is NOT about trying to sink three-pointers blindfolded to the roar of the crowd. You want to make the task as easy as possible. There are no bonus points awarded for degree of difficulty when it comes to trading. All that counts is getting that ball through the hoop as consistently as possible.

Consistency is one of the most important things you can develop as a trader, and it all comes from having the right mindset.

A consistent trader isn't constantly trying to hit home runs, they are always looking for the low-hanging fruit.

A consistent trader isn't hanging onto losing trades, hoping and praying they become good. They are ruthlessly pruning them from their trading account.

A word of warning: consistency is harder to achieve than it sounds. You see, the human brain is hardwired to seek out random rewards. That's why casinos are such a profitable business. Winning a random reward is fun. It makes us "feel clever," our ego gets a boost because we have "beaten the house," and we now have "bragging rights." This all adds up to an exciting and potentially addictive dopamine hit. In other words, our human brain finds random rewards pleasurable.

If you take this mindset into the markets, you are not asking but begging for trouble. Don't be tempted to always be looking for the next big kill and instead trade like a pro. Commit to consistency.

"Without commitment, you'll never start...without consistency, you'll never finish."

—DENZEL WASHINGTON

IF YOU CAN CHANGE YOUR FOCUS, YOU CAN CHANGE YOUR FUTURE

"Do not anticipate trouble, or worry about what may never happen. Keep in the sunlight."

—BENJAMIN FRANKLIN

Here are my tips on focus.

Don't spend a minute worrying about something you can't control. You can't control what the Fed does, what the President says, or what the unemployment rate is. You can't control what the market does. So don't worry about them. I'm not saying ignore them, but don't waste any mental real estate worrying about things you can't control.

Focus instead on becoming the best trader you can be. Do your homework, follow your process, and don't deviate from this path. Whenever I find a trade setup that I like, I prepare the equivalent of a pitch document on the trade in question, highlighting the reasons I like the trade. I then present the trade to my CEO (my higher self). On a trade-by-trade basis, I grade my performance only by how well I am following my process. The specific outcome of any individual trade is not a measure of my success or failure as a trader.

Outcomes only become relevant after dozens of trades. If you focus on adhering to a strong process and to enjoying the process of ~~sex~~ trading, the odds of a pleasing outcome are stacked in your favor.

Focus also on why you are trading. What is your own personal "why"? Want to grow your capital? Or earn a second income? Pay for kids' or grandkids' education? Escape a day job that you hate? Get super clear about and focus on your own personal "why" and this is what will keep you motivated.

Focus too on the abundance of opportunity available in the financial markets. Approximately $400 billion changes hands on US stock markets every day. Do you really think that money is scarce? It's bloody everywhere! It's natural for us to desire more money, and this desire is absolutely fine. It's why most of us get into trading in the first place. But remember, every desire has two sides. Do you believe you can manifest struggle, financial hardship, and losing trades in your life? If so, then the reverse must also be true! Always focus on what you want, rather than the absence of what you want.

AVOID DISTRACTIONS (AKA THE "NEWS")

Life these days is overrun with useless distractions that deliberately misdirect our attention. Life is literally wasted, with focus being diverted to the trivial and unimportant. If you let them, these distractions will sap your mental energy, leaving you feeling depleted. Yet much of our modern society is designed to elicit short-term emotional thinking and a reactive nature. Consider the lengths the media goes to every day to make us feel outrage, fear, and hate. Become mindful of this and you will start to notice the daily attempts to stoke your negative emotions and unmoor you.

Remember, the job of mainstream news media is to sell advertising, not to inform. They will say provocative things that are deliberately designed to keep you hanging on until after the commercial break. As human beings we are naturally drawn to fear, disaster, and gossip, causing a flood of chemicals our bodies release when we are exposed to such stimulus. Stop chasing these cheap thrills. You become what you focus on.

During my childhood and teenage years, TV news was a reasonably neutral thirty-minute report of the events of the day. It has since devolved into a 24/7 propaganda machine filled with narratives, sound bites, and talking points designed to take advantage of the fact that:

"Humans are fear-based creatures. We are primarily emotional, and our ruling emotion is fear."

—JED MCKENNA

And the volume just keeps getting turned up. Our fear and outrage are constantly being stoked. When we let these negative emotions seep into our brains unchecked, they negatively impact the quality of the decisions we make. Fear is the silent assassin to our ability to make good decisions.

Also be aware that the financial news never predicts the market. It simply reacts to what has already happened. Price will usually move before the news...and the media just scrambles in search of a story that matches the move in price after the fact.

STOP OBSESSING OVER PRICE ACTION

If you are relentlessly checking markets, obsessing over every uptick and downtick in price, you're telling your brain that this is what's important. When you do this, you allow your emotions and your ego to take over. You're likely to feel little surges of emotion when you focus obsessively over price, and this in itself can become addictive.

The ego loves nothing more than to get "busy." Hence, when obsessing over price action, we can also fall prey to the "busy" trap. We can delude ourselves into thinking that we are spending a lot of time working on something productive, when all we are really doing is distracting ourselves.

If you want to be a day trader, that's a different matter. However, day trading is not what I am teaching in this book.

MASTER YOUR OUTLOOK TOWARD UNCERTAINTY

Realize and accept that anything can happen in markets and in trading. Realize that uncertainty is the rule. We have setups that give us a strong edge, but we never *know* what is going to happen. As traders, we must accept this and embrace uncertainty.

Objectivity, impartiality, discipline, focus, courage, and belief already live within you. Grow these attributes through habit and repetition so that they dominate your thinking.

Successful traders move beyond the fear of making mistakes. They accept that lots of small losses are part and parcel of a trader's life. Successful traders instead focus on probabilities. Knowing that they have an edge and that over time the probabilities are stacked in their favor, they embrace uncertainty. They recognize that few are comfortable embracing uncertainty. And that, within the uncertainty, lies a massive pool of opportunity.

A HAPPY TRADER IS A SUCCESSFUL TRADER

Bring your best game with you when you are trading. I'm sure you've noticed how happy, self-confident people tend to perform better in the dating game than angry, fearful people. The same is true in trading. Happy, confident people tend to do well in the financial markets while angry, fearful people struggle to thrive. I'm sure there are exceptions, but this observation has been overwhelmingly true in my more than twenty-five years of experience in financial markets.

It is extremely common for people to confuse the happiness equation. People fall into the trap of thinking, "When I'm successful, then I'll be happy," or "When I'm rich, then I'll be happy." But this equation is ass-backward. If this equation were true, then only the outside environment would determine our happiness. Think for a moment about what a disempowering world that would be.

The correct formula is, "When I'm happy, then I'll be successful."

This also applies to trading. People think, "Once I'm a profitable trader, then I'll be happy." The reverse is true. "When I'm happy, then I'll be a profitable trader."

An unhappy, fearful trader has a really tough job ahead of himself to become a successful trader.

Anything you can do to foster an internal state of happiness or peace is going to boost your trading results way more than adding some fancy new indicator to your charts. Happiness I think is even too strong a word. I recommend aiming for a state of mild contentment.

Small, consistent actions to improve our happiness or state of contentment will have a significant positive effect on our trading over time. While happiness is predominantly a feeling, it is also a muscle that can be trained.

Traditional trading psychology focuses on eliminating what's bad, such as poor consistency or discipline, not following our trading plan, etc. THIS STUFF IS IMPORTANT!

But if all we do is strive to eliminate the bad, we'll end up missing out on adding in the good that will really help us exceed the average. Happiness is an important and often overlooked area in trading that I work on consistently with the traders that I coach.

Many excellent books have been written on happiness and I do not intend to try and write another book on the subject here. I will however share some of my recommendations on books that have helped me in this regard. Ironically, many of the books that have helped me the most in trading are not even about trading.

- *The Untethered Soul: The Journey Beyond Yourself* by **Michael Singer**—This book taught me to recognize that the incessant, aimless chatter inside my head isn't me. Rather, I am the *observer* of that voice in my head, who quite frankly is an asshole to me a lot of the time. This book taught me how to put some distance between the real "me" and my ego and gain a better perspective. The messages in this book are similar to Eckhart Tolle's excellent *The Power of Now*. I just found *The Untethered Soul* much easier to read and the messages more accessible.
- *Breaking the Habit of Being Yourself* by **Dr. Joe Dispenza**— We all carry around a bunch of subconscious junk that makes negative emotions habitual. Getting rid of as much of this junk as possible is highly desirable, otherwise we bring it with us into the markets. If you have feelings of shame or unworthiness for example, the markets will have a way of delivering what you subconsciously feel you deserve. You deserve the world, whether you realize that or not. Dr. Joe teaches us how to rid ourselves of negative thought patterns through a series of meditations. His other books, *You Are The Placebo: Making Your Mind Matter* and *Becoming Supernatural: How Common People Are Doing the Uncommon* are also excellent, but this book is the place to start. It's genuinely groundbreaking and potentially life-changing stuff. Highly recommended.
- *The Happiness Advantage: The Seven Principles of Positive Psychology That Fuel Success and Performance at Work* by **Shawn Achor**—Not only does Shawn teach us that happiness is an internal state we can cultivate, he teaches us HOW to do it through a series of easy-to-follow steps. Happiness really is a

muscle that we can train and exercise. An easy read and a must read in my opinion.

- *Trading In the Zone: Master the Market with Confidence, Discipline and a Winning Attitude* by **Mark Douglas**—Widely regarded as the "bible" on trading psychology, this book is a must-read for all traders of any experience level. If you have not read it, please order it as soon as you finish this book! This book has been read at least once by virtually every successful trader I know.

CHAPTER 4

SAILING WITH THE WIND AT YOUR BACK

I remember fondly my first whitewater rafting trip with my good buddy, Sam. We went rafting on the Arkansas River (which I found out that day is pronounced ar-ken-saw!) in Colorado.

It was a fun, wet, scary, thrilling, exhilarating, bouncy day. There were eight of us in the raft and everybody had a blast. I remember at the briefing the guide telling us, "Folks, this is not a Disney ride. Listen carefully to these instructions because we cannot turn the water off!"

As we were preparing to drop the raft into the river, everybody watched which way the river was flowing. And nobody thought, even for a second, about trying to paddle the raft upstream.

If only the average investor would take the trouble of paying attention to which way the market was flowing before dropping their money in.

Aspiring traders are frequently tempted into buying stocks that are falling, in the hope they'll pick a bottom (which is quite disgusting if you really think about it). People are forever struggling against the flow of the market and getting stuck in its eddies and currents, because they have never learned the proper navigation techniques. The aim of this chapter is to teach you those very navigation techniques.

THE NINTH WONDER OF THE WORLD?

If compound interest is the eighth wonder of the world (it isn't), then I firmly believe that trend following is the ninth. I will explain why in this chapter.

At its essence, trend following is determining the dominant trend of the stock you are looking to trade and following that trend, rather than fighting it.

Think of the trend as the direction of the flow of a river.

If its trend is up, you buy the stock.

If its trend is down, you sell it.

In either case, you are doing the equivalent of pointing your raft downstream rather than trying to fight the current.

Sound simple? Good, because there is no need to overcomplicate this. Remember, simpler is nearly always better.

Trend trading is all about following the path of least resistance.

It is like sailing with the wind at your back.

Or paddling your raft downstream on the Arkansas River (an admission...I still say ar-kans-as in my head when I see that word!).

WHY I LOVE TREND FOLLOWING

I love trend following. I believe every aspiring trader should learn trend following before any other trading method and make trend following their primary focus.

Why?

Let me share the many reasons with you.

- First, trends are easy to spot, when you know what to look for. And I'm going to teach you exactly how to start identifying them in this chapter.
- Second, because trends are easy to spot, trend following is highly teachable. This was proven in a famous experiment that came to be known as the "Turtle Traders." In 1983, legendary commodities' trader, Richard Dennis (who himself turned $5,000 into $100 million through trend trading) took fourteen complete beginners and taught them how to trade. Over the course of the next five years, the so-called "Turtles" produced a profit of $175 million. Dennis's experiment proved beyond a doubt that it's possible to teach trend trading.
- Third, trends often exhibit remarkable persistence. This has to do with basic human nature, which hasn't changed much over the millennia and is unlikely to do so in the foreseeable future. We will discuss this in more detail, later in this chapter.

- Fourth, when trend following, it's quite easy to determine when you are wrong on a trade. This makes risk management quite straightforward. When you are wrong on a trade, your job is to get out of the trade quickly and at a small loss. Yes, you will get some trades wrong. Losing trades are nothing more than a trader's business expense. Like any good business, we do want to keep our expenses to a minimum, which is why we always trade with an edge and follow a strong process. In terms of the various business expenses associated with trading, losing trades is the major one!
- Fifth, if you're a trend follower, you are in great company. Many of the most successful traders in the world are trend followers including many doyens of the hedge fund industry such as Bruce Kovner, Paul Tudor Jones, and Louis Bacon—all of whom are billionaires thanks to trend following. Bruce Kovner is the founder of the hedge fund, Caxton Asset Management. Not only did Kovner amass a personal fortune of over $5.5 billion, his hedge fund averaged an annual return of 21 percent per annum over a twenty-eight-year period...all thanks to trend following.

WHAT IS A TREND?

At this point you may be thinking: "Well what on earth is a trend, and how the heck do I follow one?"

Let me share with you an analogy to describe the path of a stock within a trend.

Imagine a lady walking her Jack Russell terrier on a leash, along a footpath through a park. If you look at the lady, what is she doing?

She's walking in a measured fashion, in more-or-less a straight line, just following the path. Now let your eyes pan down to watch the Jack Russell. What is the dog doing? The dog is going nuts! He's running around chasing butterflies. He's digging up clumps of mud. He's sniffing piles of rubbish and trying to hump other dogs...tugging on the leash every time a new distraction captures his attention!

The dog is going to walk in the general direction of the lady, but he is going to swing randomly and sometimes violently from one side of the footpath to the other, depending on what has caught his attention from one moment to the next.

Think of the path the lady is taking as the dominant trend of a stock. The path taken by the dog resembles the actual path taken by the stock, zigzagging back and forth around the lady (the dominant trend). The lady is following a smooth path while the dog's path is rather more erratic.

As trend followers, we need to watch both the lady and the dog. The first thing we need to do is determine what direction the lady is walking in. This is how we identify the dominant trend. Then we need to watch the dog...and wait for the dog to run into our "action zone" before we take a trade (I will explain this in chapter 7).

The definition of a trend is a prevailing tendency or inclination for something to move in a particular direction.

When it comes to trading, we are concerned with the direction that price is moving in.

The three major trends that confront traders in the market are: uptrends, downtrends, and sideways trends (or lack of trend).

When it comes to trends, a picture really is worth a thousand words.

Here is an example of a stock that is in an uptrend:

An uptrend in MA stock

Here is an example of a stock in a downtrend:

A downtrend in BLUE stock

And here is an example of a stock that isn't trending:

Lack of trend in IWM

An uptrend is evident when you can see the price chart moving consistently from the lower left to the upper right of your screen. A more formal definition of an uptrend is "a sequence of higher highs and higher lows in price."

Here is the same uptrend you saw before, but with the higher highs and higher lows highlighted:

MA is tracing out a series of higher highs and higher lows

A downtrend is the mirror image of an uptrend. Price moves from the upper left to the lower right of the screen and price is making lower highs and lower lows. Here is that downtrend example again:

BLUE is tracing out lower highs and lower lows

And a sideways trend (or no trend) is where price is fluctuating around a horizontal line and not making higher highs and higher lows or lower highs and lower lows.

Sideways trend (no trend) in IWM

HOW DO TRENDS FORM?

Let's break down these price charts into a little more detail.

If we zoom in on a chart, you will see price bars known as "candlesticks." Each candlestick shows the opening price, closing price, high price, and low price of each trading day. If the candlestick is white, that means the stock's closing price was higher than its opening price on that day. If the candlestick is black, it means the stock closed below its open.

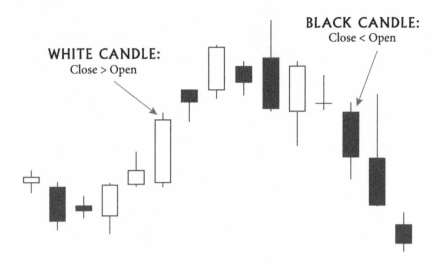

WHITE CANDLE:
Close > Open

BLACK CANDLE:
Close < Open

Each candlestick on the chart depicts the battle during that trading day between the buyers (bulls) and sellers (bears). Buyers and sellers may have many different motivations for their behavior. Let's now explore some of the most common motivations.

People who are buying the stock are usually doing so in the hope or belief it will rise in price in the future. They are optimistic about the prospects for the stock and expect these favorable prospects will be represented by a higher future stock price (i.e., they are bullish on the stock).

People who are selling the stock may expect it not to rise much in the future, so they are happy to sell their shares and lock in a profit. Alternatively, they may feel very negative about the future prospects of the company and are short selling the stock in the expectation that the poor prospects they are expecting will result in a lower stock price in the future (i.e., they are bearish on the stock).

When buyers feel strongly bullish, they buy more eagerly. Their enthusiasm to buy the stock pushes the price up.

This behavior is driven by feelings of:

- Confidence ("I've done my research and I'm sure I'm onto a good thing here. I'm going to make money on this.")
- Greed ("If this stock can rise just another $10, I'll be able to afford that holiday to Greece!")
- Euphoria ("I'm making so much money. The stock market is so easy. Everything I touch turns to gold!")
- FOMO ("All the guys at work told me about this stock last week and it's up 10 percent since then. If I don't buy now, I'm going to miss out while they're all making money!")

(By the way, if anyone ever responds to the question: "Why is stock XYZ up today?" by saying, "because there are more buyers than sellers," they're being a wise ass. All transactions that take place on the stock market are done by matching an exactly equal number of buyers and sellers. It is the increased motivation or enthusiasm of buyers that pushes the price up).

Now, when sellers feel strongly bearish, they sell more eagerly and in turn push the stock price down. This type of behavior is driven by feelings of:

- Lack of confidence ("That stock I bought last week has fallen 10 percent since I bought it. Maybe I missed something? I don't like this; I think I'll sell.")
- Fear ("I'm now down 30 percent on this position. Shit, how am I going to explain this to my wife? If it falls much further, I'll be in a margin call. I better sell now!")
- Despair ("OMG! This market has done nothing but fall for four whole weeks. I hate stocks. I wish I'd never heard of the bloody

stock market! I'm gonna kick my brother-in-law's butt for suggesting this piece of crap stock!")

- Forced Selling/margin calls

"Mr. Smith?"

"Yes?"

"It's Alex from XYZ Bank. I'm afraid your account is in a margin call. Please wire $20,000 to your account within twenty-four hours or we will be forced to sell your entire portfolio."

[drops the phone]

So, we can see that trends have their origin in strong feelings, strong human emotions.

When the trend is up, a stock's price has a strong tendency to keep rising. When this happens, people feel confident; they feel like they are looking at a moneymaker and they don't mind paying a few cents extra to get on board with a good thing.

When the trend is down, a stock's price has a strong tendency to keep falling. When this happens, people's confidence can evaporate quickly and when that happens...they do not quibble about selling at lower prices!

Waves of confidence/greed/euphoria and lack of confidence/fear/despair sweep up market players in cycles, over and over again.

"What has happened in the past will happen again. This is because Markets are driven by humans and human nature never changes."

—JESSE LIVERMORE

WHY DO TRENDS PERSIST?

"The mind projects on to the future with the expectation that the past will be repeated."

DAVID R. HAWKINS, MD/PHD

This is where things get interesting.

Because human feelings are the driver of price, trends can be *remarkably persistent.*

This is because humans are psychologically hardwired to expect that the recent past will continue into the future.

We do this all the time in our daily lives. Let me illustrate:

Imagine you're watching a ball game. Team A has hit the lead, having made the last five scoring shots in a row. Think about what the commentators are saying right now. "Team A has all the momentum!" "Team A looks unstoppable!" "Team A looks to have this game in the bag!" You can even watch the expectations that team A's recent past will continue into the future rise in real time, as bookmakers shorten their odds on team A during the game.

Or, imagine you are looking to hire somebody for a job. Two things you are likely to want to see are their Curriculum Vitae (CV) and some references. You want to see what your job applicants have done and how they have performed in the past, with the expectation that the past will repeat in the future.

A similar phenomenon plays out in the law courts. A first offender will often be treated more leniently than a repeat offender. Humans expect that someone who has offended in the past will be more likely to do so in the future, and so their crimes warrant harsher treatment.

As human beings we are constantly extrapolating the recent past into the future. Furthermore, even though we are often unconscious of it, humans love to go with the flow of the crowd—the so-called "bandwagon effect." The stock market is no exception! This is how and why trends form and how they can become extremely persistent in nature.

As a stock's uptrend persists, people's desire to get involved gets stronger; it does not fade quietly. Conversely when a downtrend persists, investors are only concerned with owning less of what's losing them money or making them look stupid. And the lower it goes, the more money it loses and the more stupid it makes them look, hence their increased desperation to sell.

Stocks that are trending strongly therefore tend to develop strong *momentum*. And anything with strong momentum—whether it's a freight train, a sports team, or a stock—is going to be hard to stop.

If we can spot a good trend—given the right set of circumstances—we can form a reasonable expectation that the trend will persist into the future. We can then exploit patterns that form within the trend for profit. Good or *good*?

TRENDSPOTTING

"Price makes news, not the other way around. A market is going to go where a market is going to go."

—PETER BORISH

We identify trends by using technical analysis.

Technical analysis is not as *technical* as it sounds. And the way I teach it, technical analysis is very *visual*.

Technical analysis is the study of price changes over time using price charts, and often, some helpful visual indicators. In the previous section, you learned how price trends have their evolution in strong human emotions. If technical analysis is the study of price changes, you can see how, at its essence, technical analysis is really the study of human behavior. Specifically, the behavior of crowds with respect to the strong emotions of fear and euphoria.

Josh Brown of The Reformed Broker blog defined a technical analyst almost perfectly:

> A technician is someone who cuts right to the chase and studies *actual* prices and behavior instead of puzzling over *the causes* of prices and behavior like everyone else.

Josh goes on to say:

> Discussing causes is a much more interesting conversation and it gets you on all the talk shows. Discussing price—the sum total of all investor fear and greed, both historical and real-time— tells you the truth about what's actually going on, it does not

offer an opinion. Besides, price dictates what the news is, not the other way around.

Price creates reality for investors, because investors take their behavioral cues from price—i.e., they buy or sell, pushing price either up or down. The media then fashions headlines from the resulting price action (up or down) and the finance industry fashions forecasts around it.

This is how we end up with chief investment strategists raising and lowering their year-end index targets for the stock market in reaction to the market rising and falling throughout the year.

It is also why we find that a stock analyst's target price for a stock they research will nearly always lag the stock price rather than lead it. They will start out with a view, and then alter that view to more closely match the reality that is being generated by price.

If an analyst starts the year with a $100 price target for MSFT, and MSFT stock happily sails up to $140, chances are she will upgrade her price target to something higher ($140? $160?) *after* the price has rallied.

Conversely if the analyst started the year with a price target of $400 on NFLX, he risks looking a bit silly (and potentially losing his job) if he maintains that price target after the price has dropped to $300. In this case, the price target gets downgraded to something lower, and closer to the reality that price offers.

When strategists and analysts change their forecasts and price targets, they will of course use fundamental developments—or the news of the day—to justify their changes. They will never admit the reason for the upgrade is because the price went up! But what they are really doing is extrapolating what's recently happened, into the future. You can't blame them, they're human after all.

This upgrade/downgrade nonsense goes on *all the time* and it's actually a standing joke among many industry insiders.

To summarize, technical analysis is simply the study of price action. It is used by nearly all market participants, whether they admit to being technicians or not. Anybody who checks a price chart before making an investment or trading decision is employing technical analysis to some extent.

BACK TO TRENDSPOTTING

Remember those charts we looked at earlier? We were identifying higher highs and higher lows in the case of an uptrend. And lower highs and lower lows in the case of a downtrend. That was already basic technical analysis!

Now, I want to introduce you to some indicators we use on our price charts to make identifying a trend even easier. Manually drawing circles and zigzags on charts is inefficient!

The first of the technical indicators I want to discuss with you are called moving averages.

Moving averages are one of the most common and simple indicators used in technical analysis.

The main function of a moving average is to smooth out price action by filtering out the "noise" from random, short-term price fluctuations.

Moving averages are the best indicators for gauging the direction of a trend because of their power and simplicity to smooth out price direction in trending markets. They create lines on your charts to filter out the daily trading ranges and show the true direction the price is heading for a specific time frame. If price is akin to the dog zigzagging back and forth across a path in the earlier analogy, think of moving averages as the smoother path taken by the lady walking the dog.

When price is going up, moving averages rise as an ascending line. When price is going down then moving averages fall as a descending line. Moving averages can also show that a market is not trending in any direction when they are flat or horizontal. Moving averages serve as great filters of the noise of intraday price action and really help to simplify the trendspotting process.

Two of the most common types of moving average indicators are simple moving averages and exponential moving averages. I use both, but I use them for slightly different purposes.

A simple moving average (SMA) is formed by calculating the average closing price of a security over a specified fixed time period (e.g., number of days). For example, a 50-day SMA is simply the average of the last 50 days' closing prices. Each day, the average is recalculated, taking into account only the closing prices of the 50 most recent daily closes.

Here is how a 50-day SMA looks on a price chart:

MA chart with the 50-day SMA added.

Notice how the path taken by price looks quite jagged and "noisy"—like the path taken by the dog in our earlier example. While the path taken by the 50-day SMA looks relatively smooth—like the path taken by the lady. An upward sloping 50 SMA line tells us that the medium-term trend for the stock is up.

An exponential moving average (EMA) applies greater weight in its calculation to more recent prices, compared to an SMA. An SMA will tend be smoother than an EMA but the SMA will lag in price more. An EMA will track price more closely than an SMA.

I like to use EMAs to help identify short-term trends. SMAs can also aid in trend identification, but I also like to use them to highlight potential areas of support and resistance (more on this in chapter 6).

HOW I DEFINE A TREND WITH EXPONENTIAL MOVING AVERAGES

OK, let's start putting some of this knowledge into practice!

For trend identification, I use EMAs with five different time periods. Those time periods are: 8, 21, 34, 55 and 89 days.

When looking for trends on a chart, I define a strong uptrend as a situation where:

- The 8 EMA is above the 21 EMA
- The 21 EMA is above the 34 EMA
- The 34 EMA is above the 55 EMA
- The 55 EMA is above the 89 EMA

Here's how they all look on a chart:

A chart of MSFT with EMAs stacked in a bullish fashion.

In the chart above, the thinnest, faintest line closest to price is the 8 EMA and the darkest, heaviest line is the 89 EMA.

This is what I call "bullish stacked EMAs" and it represents a stock that is in a strong uptrend.

Notice how when price is in an uptrend, price tends to spend the majority of its time above the EMAs. When you see a chart with stacked EMAs like this, the stock is in a strong uptrend and the path of least resistance for price is most likely higher.

A downtrend is the mirror image of an uptrend. A strong downtrend is a situation where the EMAs are stacked in the reverse order:

- The 89 EMA is above the 55 EMA
- The 55 EMA is above the 34 EMA
- The 34 EMA is above the 21 EMA
- The 21 EMA is above the 8 EMA

Here's an example of how this bearish arrangement looks on a chart:

A chart of TDC with EMAs stacked in a bearish fashion.

Notice how, when price is in a downtrend, price tends to spend most of its time below the EMAs. In a similar fashion, when we see the EMAs stacked in a bearish fashion like this, we are looking at a strong downtrend, where the path of least resistance for price is most likely to be lower.

TREND CHECKLIST

Let's put our trend identification tools into a checklist:

Uptrend:

1. Price is moving from the lower left to the upper right of the screen
2. Price is making higher highs and higher lows
3. EMAs are as follows: 8 EMA > 21 EMA > 34 EMA > 55 EMA > 89 EMA
4. Price spends most of its time above the EMAs

Downtrend:

1. Price is moving from the upper left to the lower right of the screen
2. Price is making lower highs and lower lows
3. EMAs are as follows: 8 EMA < 21 EMA < 34 EMA < 55 EMA < 89 EMA
4. Price spends most of its time below the EMAs

Congratulations! You are now a trend-spotter!

In the next chapter we will discuss trend analysis in more detail, and in chapter 6 we will explore the concept of support and resistance.

CHAPTER 5

HOW TO READ PRICE ACTION LIKE A BOOK

"My metric for everything I look at is the 200-day moving average of closing prices. I've seen too many things go to zero, stocks and commodities. The whole trick in investing is: 'How do I keep from losing everything?' If you use the 200-day moving average rule, then you get out. You play defense, and you get out."

—PAUL TUDOR JONES

In the previous chapter, we discussed the basics of how to identify a strong trend, using a combination of price action and moving averages.

In this chapter we are going to dig a little deeper into trend analysis. By the end of this chapter, you will be developing the ability to recognize high probability entry points for a trade within seconds, just by eyeballing a stock price chart.

THE FIVE HALLMARKS OF A STRONG TREND

There are five key elements I look for to assess the strength of a trend. In the following sections we will explore both uptrends and downtrends together, as it is essential that you are able to navigate both rising and falling markets.

The five hallmarks of a **strong uptrend** are as follows:

1. Price is making higher highs and higher lows.
2. Price is making steady retracements, not violent pullbacks.
3. EMAs are stacked in a neat fashion with the 8 EMA on top and the 89 EMA on the bottom.
4. Where is price relative to the moving averages? Above the 50 SMA is best.
5. The trend has been in place for at least four months.

In the case of an uptrend, I will award the trend bonus points if price **is** within 10 percent of its all-time high. These are the most bullish stocks in the market, with the least amount of "baggage." We will explore this concept further later in this chapter.

1. PRICE IS MAKING HIGHER HIGHS AND HIGHER LOWS

This is straightforward and we have covered it in the previous chapter. However just to keep building those neural networks in your brain, here is another graphical example of the type of pattern we are looking for:

A strong uptrend in MCD, with price clearly making higher highs and higher lows.

Stacked EMAs do a decent job of indicating a strong trend, but sometimes you can see stacked EMAs with a fairly flat trend. This isn't bad, per se, but it is preferable to see some slope or gradient on both the price chart AND the EMAs.

In the chart of Monster Beverage below, the EMAs are stacked in a bullish manner, but the trend is less convincing as price is NOT making higher highs.

MNST price has stopped making higher highs, even though the EMAs are stacked.

...and sure enough, the uptrend in MNST did not continue. This is why you should not rely solely on indicators when analyzing trends. Price is always the final arbiter.

The uptrend in MNST quickly comes to an end after price stops making higher highs.

Price making higher highs and higher lows is the fundamental definition of an uptrend and should be the first thing we look for.

2. PRICE IS MAKING STEADY RETRACEMENTS, NOT VIOLENT PULLBACKS

Price never moves in a straight line. This makes trading confusing at times, but this uncertainty is also the very reason trading opportunities exist in the first place.

Stock prices "breathe" in and out. There is usually a natural "wave-like" movement to price.

Even when a stock is in an uptrend, price will go through periods when it falls. In an uptrend, these periods of falling prices tend to be shorter and shallower than the periods during which prices rise. These periods of falling prices during an uptrend are called retracements, or pullbacks. They are *countertrend* moves (i.e., price moves that are *counter* to the dominant trend).

The reason these pullbacks can cause confusion is because we can never be 100 percent certain that the pullback isn't the start of a change in trend.

But because trends tend to be persistent, these pullbacks can often represent great buying opportunities in the context of an uptrend.

In a healthy uptrend, we ideally want to see orderly, measured, steady pullbacks like in the example below:

A chart of TEAM, with major pullbacks highlighted. We want to see steady, orderly, measured pullbacks like these in a strong trend.

What we want to avoid is violent pullbacks like these:

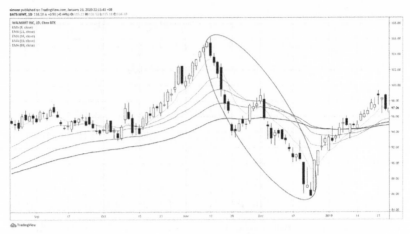

An example of a violent countertrend move in WMT, not what we want to see in a strong trend.

The converse is also true for a stock that is in a downtrend. When a stock is trending down, the countertrend moves involve price rising (rallying) as can be seen in the chart below.

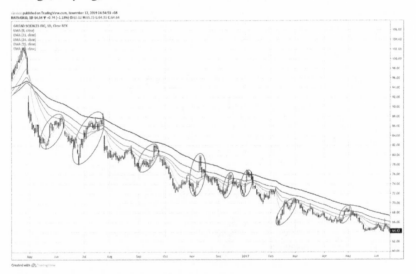

Countertrend rallies are highlighted in this strong downtrend in GILD.

Downtrends and indeed bear markets have a different *personality* from uptrends (bull markets). These retracements (this time, rallies within a downtrend) can often be quite sharp as they are often the result of short covering.

Short Selling and Short Covering

Let me briefly explain what short selling and short covering is.

Most people understand intuitively that to make money in the stock market you need to buy low and sell high. And the most intuitive way to do this is to buy something when its price is low and sell it when its price is higher. However, the buy and sell transactions don't have to be done in that order.

We can also make money in stocks by selling when the price is high first, and then buying back when the price is lower. When this is done in the stock market, the transaction is called short selling.

In short selling, a trader opens a position by first borrowing shares of a stock that she believes will fall in price. The trader then sells these shares on the market to buyers who are happy to pay the market price. The trader who sold the borrowed shares, must return these shares at some point in the future. To do so, they must first buy back the shares that they initially sold.

If the shares have fallen in price during the time in which they were sold and bought back, the short seller makes money. If the stock price has rallied, the short seller will lose money.

Here's an example. Let's say stock XYZ is trading at $55 and I think the price is due to fall. I borrow 100 shares and sell them on the market for $55. I receive proceeds of $5,500 from the sale.

If the XYZ stock price falls to $50, I can "cover my short" by buying the 100 shares back at $50. This will cost me $5,000 which is $500 less than what I sold them for. This leaves me with a profit of $500 on the trade, less any stock borrow and transaction fees I must pay.

Of course, if the XYZ stock price rallies to $60 I will lose money on the trade. To cover my short position, I must buy the 100 shares back at $60, which will cost me $6,000. Since I only received $5,500 for the initial sale of the shares, I am $500 out of pocket on the trade (not including stock borrow and transaction fees).

So short covering is the buy transaction that closes a short sale of stock. Sometimes stocks can become heavily shorted, for one reason or another. If a stock has a high level of short interest (i.e., a large percentage of the issued stock has been sold short) and its price starts to rise, a short-covering rally can ensue. This is when short sellers scramble to cover their short positions to lock in gains, or to manage risk on a position that is moving into a loss.

Short covering rallies can be fast and furious, particularly in stocks with high short interest. Violent moves against the trend are therefore rather more common in a bear market. Options offer us an easier, lower risk way of taking a short position in a stock. We can mimic a short position in a stock by buying put options, to profit from falling stock prices. We will cover this in detail in chapters 8 through 10.

3. EMAS ARE STACKED IN A NEAT FASHION

A great indicator of a strong trend is EMAs that are stacked in a neat fashion. We want to see the EMAs laid out in a rainbow-like fashion as in the charts below:

EMAs for NKE are stacked in a neat fashion.

I have a thirteen-year-old daughter who was obsessed with rainbows as a little girl. On the color charts that I use on my PC, I even color my moving averages according to the colors of the rainbow (you can view examples of the color charts I use at https://taooftrading.com/bookbonus).

We generally want to avoid trading any chart where the EMAs look like twisted rope, as in the example below:

4. WHERE IS PRICE RELATIVE TO THE MOVING AVERAGES? ABOVE THE 50 SMA IS BEST

Where price sits in relation to the moving averages is also important and can provide valuable clues as to where price may be heading next.

As discussed previously, exponential moving averages (EMAs) track current price action more closely. I find them very helpful in determining the trend of the stock—particularly shorter-term trends. The three EMAs I plot on my charts are the 8, the 21, and the 34 period EMAs.

The EMAs can also act as minor levels of support (in the case of an uptrend) and resistance (in the case of a downtrend).

Simple moving averages (SMAs) can also be used to determine trend, and they can also identify potentially stronger levels of support and resistance.

When a stock is trading right on its 50 SMA or its 200 SMA, it is effectively having a giant spotlight beamed on it. Institutional investors (like pension funds, mutual funds, and hedge funds) look at and use the 50 SMA and 200 SMA to assess potential entry and exit points. When stocks reach these levels, you can be certain they are receiving a lot of attention and many investors will have reached a major decision point regarding the stock in question.

My main trading chart has the following moving averages plotted on it:

8 EMA	
21 EMA	Used to determine short-term trend and support/resistance
34 EMA	
50 SMA	Use to gauge medium-term trend. Important area of potential support or resistance
100 SMA	Last line of defense before the stock finds its way back to the 200 SMA
200 SMA	The line-in-the-sand between a long-term uptrend and a long-term downtrend. Also, a potentially important level of support or resistance

This is how they look on a chart:

A chart of V, with all the key EMAs (dashed lines) and SMAs (solid lines) plotted.

The dotted/dashed lines in the chart above are the 8 EMA, 21 EMA, and 34 EMA. They track price quite closely and are helpful in identifying the short- to medium-term trend and areas of potential short-term support (or resistance, in the case of a downtrend).

The solid lines are the 50 SMA, the 100 SMA, and the 200 SMA.

The 50 SMA highlights the medium-term trend and often acts as a strong area of support (or resistance, in the case of a downtrend). The 200 SMA defines the long-term trend and is often regarded as the line in the sand between a bull market and a bear market. The 100 SMA can also act as support, but I use this line less often. My strong preference is to trade stocks that are at or above their 50 SMA in an uptrend, and at or below their 50 SMA in a downtrend.

5. THE TREND HAS BEEN IN PLACE FOR AT LEAST FOUR MONTHS

The best trends to trade are those that are well established. As we saw in chapter 2, trends owe their existence and their persistence to human nature. When market participants see that a stock has been going up for a long period of time, their desire to get involved in that stock increases. It doesn't decrease, as our logical brains might expect. No, the stock market is one of the few places on earth where demand for something increases as its price increases!

A stock that is only in the early stages of an uptrend tends to be more unpredictable. When considering a trend trade in a stock, I like to see that the trend has been in place for at least four months and that there has already been at least one pullback—that is, one move counter to the dominant trend—that price has managed to recover from.

Stocks that have at least a few months' worth of movement predominantly in one direction make better trend trading candidates. A trend in its infancy can easily falter and reverse. A stock that has been trending in one direction for several months or years is more likely to keep going in that direction. This runs counter to the intuition of most people. When we see a stock that has been trending up for a couple of years, we are tempted to think "its run must be over, surely it can't keep rising from here." The fact is that stocks and even stock markets can trend for years!

The dominant trend of the S&P 500 has been up for over 10 years!

Price Is within 10 Percent of Its All-Time High

Many aspiring traders are wary of stocks that are trading near their all-time highs. "Surely, it can't go any higher" is their instinct. But thinking this way will really trip you up in trading. Stocks that are making new highs are the most bullish stocks in the market and they are the very stocks we want to be focusing on for potential bullish trades. Think about it like this: when a stock makes a new all-time high, *everybody who owns that stock is making money!* Anyone who doesn't own that stock is *kicking themselves!*

When a stock is making new highs, no one is thinking: "Man, if this stock can just get back to $100, I'll sell and be able to break even on my position."

A stock trading at all-time highs has none of that baggage. It's in clear air. Every single person who owns that stock is making money! Think about the psychology at work here. Everybody who holds the stock is happy, excited, and wondering how much higher it can go. Nobody is desperately waiting for the stock to get back to their original entry price so they can sell without making a loss. People who don't hold the stock are keen to get involved and will likely buy any dip. These are some of the best stocks to trade from the bullish side.

The momentum factor—the tendency for winning stocks to keep winning and losing stocks to keep losing—is one of the best documented factors in equity markets. As traders, we want to be buying the best performers and shorting the worst performers. We want exposure to stocks with momentum.

There can be a temptation among novice traders to buy laggards, in the hope or expectation they will play catchup. This is a losing strategy if you are trading options. As traders, we want to buy the strongest stocks in the strongest sectors and short the weakest stocks in the weakest sectors. Our objective is to make consistent short-term gains from the market using options, and stocks that offer strong momentum are the best candidates. Buy what is already going up. Don't buy what is falling in the hope that it will change directions and start going up. This is a lower percentage strategy, given the time and energy required to change a stock's direction.

We are not trying to copy Warren Buffett or be long-term value investors. I'm not saying that's a *bad* strategy. It's just an inappropriate strategy for someone looking to grow their account quickly or generate consistent, frequent cash flow from the stock market.

Let's Talk about Downtrends

Yes, stocks can and do fall in price and enter downtrends too! So, it's important that we learn to identify downtrends so that we can be profitable traders even during a bear market.

The five hallmarks of a **strong downtrend** are as follows:

1. Price is making lower highs and lower lows.
2. Price is making steady retracements, not violent pullbacks.
3. Moving averages are stacked in a neat fashion with the 89 EMA on top and the 8 EMA on the bottom.
4. Where is price relative to the moving averages? Below the 50 SMA is best.
5. The trend has been in place for at least one month.

Here is the chart of Gilead Sciences again, illustrating a strong downtrend with EMAs stacked in a bearish fashion:

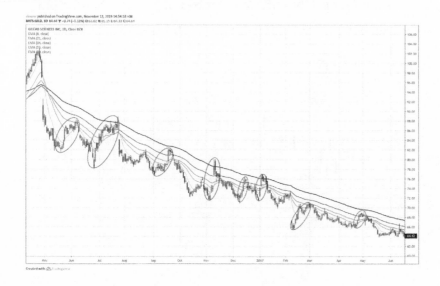

The hallmarks are mostly the same as for an uptrend but reversed.

The one exception is the amount of time the trend has been in place. I am happy to start looking for short opportunities in a stock as soon as the 8 EMA has crossed under the 34 EMA (more on this in the summary below). Stocks often spend less time in downtrends than they do in uptrends. A downtrend may not always last for as long as four months.

SUMMARY: KEY GUIDELINES FOR DETERMINING A TREND

The following is a summary of the guidelines I have developed to determine the trend in price, respecting the interaction between price and the key moving averages.

When the 8 EMA crosses up through the 34 EMA from below, this is confirmation of a short-term uptrend. This is when we start buying retracements, "buying the dip" (see point A in the chart below). When the 8 EMA crosses below the 34 EMA from above, this is confirmation of a short-term downtrend. This is when we start shorting rallies, "selling the rip" (see point B in the chart below).

At point A, the 8 EMA crosses above the 34 EMA, indicating a short-term uptrend. At point B, the 8 EMA crosses below the 34 EMA indicating a short-term downtrend.

- In a very strong uptrend, price will often find support around the 8 EMA.
- In a strong uptrend, price will often find support around the 21 EMA.
- In a moderate uptrend, price will often find support around the 34 EMA.
- In a very strong downtrend, price will often find resistance around the 8 EMA.
- In a strong downtrend, price will often find resistance around the 21 EMA.
- In a moderate downtrend, price will often find resistance around the 34 EMA.

The 50 SMA is a key level of potential support that many market participants focus on. When price reaches the 50 SMA, you can be sure a lot of professional investors who control billions of dollars' worth of investment funds are paying attention. And if they are paying attention to it, we should be too! Price hitting the 50 SMA often means billions of dollars of investment capital are making a decision to add to or cut a position on the stock in question.

Shaded areas show COST finding support at the 50 SMA.

The 100 SMA is what I call "the last line of defense" before price finds its way all the way back to the 200 SMA. The 100 SMA can often act as support or resistance, but I have found the 50 SMA and the 200 SMA work as stronger areas of support/resistance. If price breaks the 100 SMA (defined as two closes on the other side of the line), the probability is high that price will find its way all the way back to the 200 SMA.

The 200 SMA is the "line in the sand" between a bull market and a bear market. When price is trading above the 200 SMA, it is generally in a long-term uptrend where we are looking to buy dips. When price falls below the 200 SMA, volatility usually picks up and we enter a longer-term "sell the rip" environment.

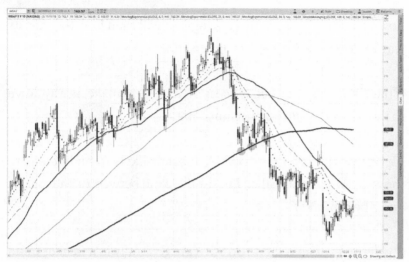

Shaded circles show WDAY initially finding support at the 200 SMA, but once this level is breached, the downtrend is confirmed.

Imagine all of the moving average lines are fences in a paddock, and price is a herd of cattle.

The herd of cattle will walk up to the first fence (the 8 EMA) and try and push it over. If the fence is strong enough to withstand the push of the herd, the cattle will go back to whatever they were doing previously (i.e., price will go back to trending).

If, however, the herd is strong enough to push over the first fence (i.e., price is strong enough to break through the 8 EMA), the cattle will then make their way to the second fence (the 21 EMA). If the second fence can withstand their push, the herd will go back to whatever it was doing previously. If, however, the herd can push through the second fence (the 21 EMA), they will make their way to the third fence (i.e., price will find its way to the 34 EMA) and try pushing against that.

If price can push its way through the 34 EMA (i.e., the cattle push down the third fence in this analogy), it will then look to make its way to the 50 SMA and push against that.

If the 50 SMA is breached, price is then likely to make its way down to the 100 SMA and push against that.

If price can breach the 100 SMA it is now likely to find its way to the 200 SMA, the so-called line-in-the-sand between a bull market and a bear market.

Stocks that are near their 100 SMA are generally in a weaker trend environment and can therefore be more unpredictable. I prefer trend trading stocks that are respecting the 50 SMA line.

To summarize:

1st fence	8 EMA	If price breaks through, prices heads to 21 EMA
2nd Fence	21 EMA	If price breaks through, next target is the 34 EMA
3rd Fence	34 EMA	If price breaks through, next target is the 50 SMA
4th Fence	50 SMA	If price breaks through, next target is the 100 SMA
5th Fence	100 SMA	If price breaks through, next target is the 200 SMA
6th Fence	200 SMA	If price breaks through this level, we are on notice that the long-term trend has probably changed

I define a breach of any of the MA lines as two consecutive closes on the other side of the line. For example, if a stock is in an uptrend and I see two closes below the 21 EMA, I am expecting price to work its way down to the 34 EMA. If a stock is in a downtrend and I see two closes above the 34 EMA, I am expecting price to make its way back up to the 21 EMA.

The moving average lines have far more power as levels of potential support or resistance when the lines have some slope or gradient to them. That is, moving averages will tend to hold price provided they are diagonal. When a moving average line is flat/horizontal, this tells us that there is no trend on that time period. Price is more likely to ignore horizontal moving average lines, pushing through them as if they weren't even there.

CHAPTER 6

WHERE AND WHY PRICE GETS "STUCK"

It's now time for us to explore the concepts of support and resistance. They are important concepts that when used properly, can significantly increase our edge in trading. This chapter will explain all of the essentials as to how and why support and resistance works.

Support and resistance are price zones on a chart where price tends to get "stuck."

Support is an area where price tends to stop falling, while resistance is an area where price tends to stop rising. Support has the effect of placing a floor beneath price while resistance acts like a price ceiling.

One of the key concepts in technical analysis is that price has *memory*. This is because humans (who make up the market) are susceptible to "anchoring bias." This bias is a human tendency to place too much emphasis on an initial piece of information acquired when making decisions and then using that information to make future decisions.

When it comes to the stock market, people anchor themselves to the price they initially paid for a stock. They tend to base future decisions about the stock based on their purchase price. For example, assume someone buys a stock at a support level of $100. The stock subsequently falls, and trades around $85-$90 for a while. Often, the people who bought at $100 will be keen to sell the stock if it manages to rally back to $100. They feel relieved that they can get out of the position at breakeven. This is their ego's attempt to protect them from experiencing the shame of a loss.

Support and resistance will swap roles. A support level once broken, will tend to become a resistance level, as we saw with the $100 price level in the previous paragraph. A resistance level, once breached, will become a support level.

Support and resistance can be illustrated by horizontal lines or diagonal lines, straight lines or wiggly lines. Even though people often draw lines on a chart to show support and resistance, it's important to remember that support and resistance are never as precise as a thin line. They are always a zone, or region, on your chart.

With all this in mind, let's look at the important ways we can identify high probability areas of support and resistance on a price chart.

MOVING AVERAGES

Moving averages often act as an area of support or resistance for a stock. As we saw in the previous chapter, a stock that is in a very strong uptrend will often find support at its 8 period EMA. A stock in a strong uptrend will often find support at its 21 EMA. I often think of the 34 EMA as the line between a stock in a fast uptrend and a stock in a moderate uptrend. The 34 EMA is another area where a stock can find support.

A stock that is in a very strong downtrend will often find resistance at its 8 period EMA. Because stocks tend to fall much more quickly than they rise, you don't always see rallies back up to the 21 EMA, 34 EMA, or 50 SMA, but these levels can also act as good levels of resistance if reached by a downtrending stock.

The 50 period and 200 period simple moving averages (SMAs) are key areas of potential support and resistance that institutional investors pay heed to. The 50 SMA can often act as a strong level of support or resistance. As I have noted previously, the 200-day SMA is widely regarded as the "line in the sand" between an uptrend and a downtrend.

If a stock that has been in an uptrend breaks below its 200 SMA, the performance of the stock usually worsens, its volatility usually rises, and it has likely entered a longer-term downtrend.

When a stock trades at its 200 SMA, it has reached a significant technical decision point. Many market players are deciding whether to add to the position or cut it. It's usually either a great buying opportunity or a great selling opportunity! Stocks that are trading at their 200 SMA are receiving plenty of attention. It's an important level that most market players pay attention to.

The 100 SMA is another moving average that I do plot on my charts, but I don't trade off it very often. If a stock breaches the 100 SMA, I know that more often than not, it is lining up a date with the 200 SMA in the future.

My favorite trend continuation trades are those where the stock bounces off its 8 EMA, 21 EMA, 34 EMA, or 50 SMA. Stocks that are trading at their 200 SMA require more finesse and they tend to be slower to move. The stock has generally lost a lot of momentum by the time it reaches the 200 SMA.

For me to consider a moving average to have been broken by price, I need to see two consecutive closes in the opposite direction. For example, if a stock is in an uptrend, I need to see two consecutive closes below the 21 EMA before I consider that EMA to have been breached.

When identifying potential areas of support and resistance using moving averages, it is also important to consider the "personality" of the stock in question.

Some stocks will test their 21 EMA time and again and you will rarely see a sharper pullback than that. Other stocks will routinely test their 50 SMA on pullbacks. You need to be aware of this if you are contemplating buying a pullback to the 21 EMA for example.

STRAIGHT LINES ON THE CHART

First, I want to define the terminology I use when talking about support and resistance lines drawn in a chart.

Horizontal regions on a chart where price gets stuck are what I refer to as support and resistance. For example:

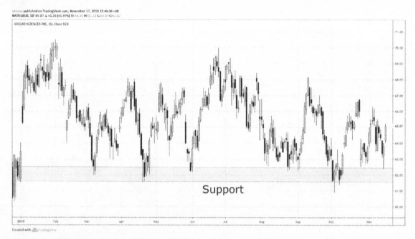

The chart highlights a support zone in GILD.

Chart highlighting a resistance zone in MSFT.

"Double bottoms" (and the even rarer "triple bottoms") are bullish reversal signals where price will test a region of support twice (or three times) before reversing bullishly. The bearish equivalent are "double tops" and "triple tops."

Both a double top and a double bottom are highlighted in the chart below.

A double top and a double bottom are highlighted on this CVS chart.

There is a common misconception in technical analysis that the more times price tests support or resistance, the stronger it becomes. Ah, if only life—and trading—was so simple.

The truth is multiple tests of a horizontal support or resistance line are more likely to have the effect of weakening that support or resistance over time.

Have a look at the chart below:

Resistance becomes an area of support that is tested multiple times in this chart of gold futures.

Notice how in the above chart, price stops falling at support (indicated by the shaded region and the arrows). This is because lots of people have noticed where the support level is and have placed buy orders at or around that support level. This means there is buying pressure around that support level to push prices higher. Now, if the market keeps re-testing that support level, all those buy orders will eventually get filled.

And when all the buy orders have been filled and there are no more buy orders left, what do you think will happen to price?

Let's look at the same chart again, but we'll zoom out to the right to see what happens.

Resistance becomes support and becomes resistance again.

Pro tip: don't fall into the trap of assuming that just because a price zone has acted as support multiple times in the past, it will continue to act as support forever.

There is an old saying in technical analysis "*there's no such thing as a quadruple bottom.*" What this means is, once price has tested a support level four times, look for it to break down on the fifth test. I wouldn't treat this statement as 100 percent definitive, but it has certainly proven to be a useful rule of thumb in my trading.

Just like Jamie Lee Curtis and Lindsay Lohan in the movie *Freaky Friday*, support and resistance will swap roles. That is, previous resistance will often become support when price breaks through it, and previous support is likely to become resistance when price breaks below it. This role-swapping can be seen clearly in the chart above.

TREND LINES

Diagonal lines on a chart that contain price are what I refer to as trend lines.

A trend line is a line drawn on a chart that connects previous spots where price has paused and turned around. They represent regions that have prevented a stock's price from moving higher (resistance) or lower (support). I find trend lines can be a useful form of supplementary analysis and can help strengthen the case for a trade, however I rarely take a trade based on trend lines alone.

An uptrend in the NASDAQ.

A downtrend in TWLO.

You need to be able to connect at least two points to create a trend line (duh). But a trend line with only two points of connection can be easily broken. A diagonal trend line with three or four points of connection will have greater validity. Unlike horizontal support and resistance lines, multiple tests of a trend line will strengthen it.

TREAT TREND LINES ALSO AS A ZONE

A common mistake that traders make is treating trend lines like a precise instrument.

A common question I get from novice traders is: "Should I draw trend lines for the candle wicks or the candle bodies?" There is some subjectivity involved in drawing a trend line. The key thing to remember is that trend lines should be drawn in a manner that connects the most possible key price points, even if the trend line ignores some "spindles."

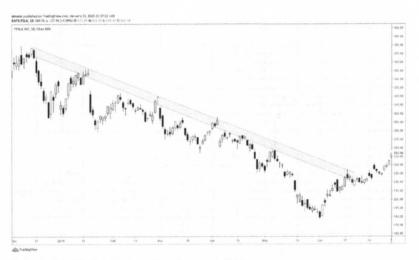

Resistance identified by a downward trending zone in TSLA.

If I have drawn a trend line on my charts, I want to see two consecutive closes on the other side of the trend line to confirm a break of the trend line, much the same as I do with moving average lines.

For example, if we have a line of resistance on our chart, we want to see a close above the trend line and then a subsequent higher close to confirm a breakout above resistance. If we don't wait for this confirmation, we greatly increase our risk of falling for false breakouts.

A false breakout occurs when price appears to break a trend line, only to reverse direction.

Unfortunately, you and I are not the only people looking at support and resistance levels. These levels are usually quite obvious to other players in the market. A false breakout could be thought of as an attempt to deceive novice traders into thinking price is going to continue to move in a certain direction, only for it to sharply reverse.

I teach people to only buy call or put options after a reversion to the mean (this is explained in chapter 7). The way I trade and the way I teach people to trade, false breakouts are never a problem. But given the power of false breakouts, let's take a look at what they are and how they work.

FALSE BREAKOUTS

Probably the best example of a false breakout in recent memory was the false breakout in crude oil, following the drone attack on Saudi oil fields in September 2019.

Crude oil futures had been in a downtrend since October 2018. However, following the news of the drone attacks, oil futures surged on the expectation of supply shortages.

Traders saw the price of crude oil futures break out of a long-term downtrend line at around $58 and aggressively bought the break-out, expecting the price surge would continue. This buying of the breakout caused crude to surge all the way to ~$64 in the space of twenty-four hours. This was an explosive move to the upside.

A few days after the attacks, it was announced that supply disruptions would be minimal, and it would be pretty much business as usual for oil markets after all. The oil price started to fall in response.

Now, when the price of crude oil futures fell back below the level where it initially broke out (around $58), all the traders who had bought the breakout were trapped in a losing position. They were what we call "trapped longs." As the oil price continued to fall below $58, traders who had bought the breakout bailed out of their long positions as their stop-losses were hit. This selling from "trapped longs" exacerbated the short-term fall in the price of oil, and helped the price accelerate back down to the $51 level over the next week.

Whenever a large number of traders are "trapped" on the wrong side of a move, this will have the effect of magnifying a move in the opposite direction of the failed breakout.

The failed breakout in crude oil futures is highlighted by the grey oval in this chart.

ROUND NUMBERS

Believe it or not, round numbers often act as support and resistance. By round numbers I mean numbers that are multiples of one hundred, fifty, ten, and twenty-five. This is just another example of humans behaving like the emotional creatures they are. "I'll sell my Microsoft shares if they get to $150!" or "I'll buy Netflix if it pulls back to $300!"

Look at how many times GOOGL touched the $1,000 price level.

Round numbers often act as support and resistance. See how many times GOOGL paused right near the $1,000 level.

A similar phenomenon is exhibited here with Chevron. Notice how much work the stock has done around the $100 price level:

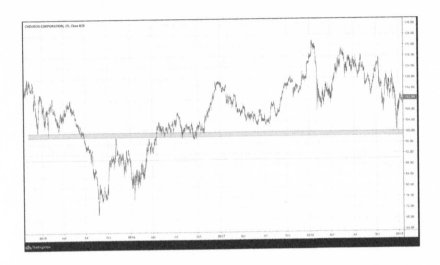

FIBONACCI LEVELS

If you think back to your high school math classes, you may remember the Fibonacci sequence.

The sequence goes: 0, 1, 1, 2, 3, 5, 8, 13, 21, 34, 55, 89, 144, 233, 377... on into infinity.

Each new number in the series is formed by adding the previous two numbers, for example:

8+21 = 34

21+34 = 55, and so on.

Some of those numbers may look familiar to you. We use the 8, 21, 34, 55 and 89 numbers for our EMAs to determine trends.

We also use ratios derived from the number series in trading.

What is truly fascinating about the Fibonacci number series is that there is a constant ratio found within the series as it progresses toward infinity.

In the relationship between the numbers in the series, you will find that the ratio is 0.618. This ratio is often referred to as the Golden Ratio, or Divine Proportion, or Golden Mean.

Take any two consecutive numbers in the series (after you get beyond the first few), divide the smaller number by the larger one that follows, and you will find the Golden Ratio. For example, 55 / 89 = 0.618, and 144 is 61.8 percent greater than 89, etc.

We use the Golden Ratio, as well as other ratios derived from the number series to identify areas of support and resistance. These Fibonacci ratios help us to identify high probability price levels where we can enter trades with an increased edge.

We can use Fibonacci ratios to find support and resistance and also to forecast price targets and expected areas of trend exhaustion.

Price has a strong tendency to get "stuck" at or very near Fibonacci levels. Have a look at the chart of the S&P 500 below and notice how price tends to pause at the key Fibonacci ratios (indicated by horizontal lines).

In this chart we can see the S&P 500 finding support and resistance at key Fibonacci levels.

Fibonacci levels provide me with a significant additional edge in my trading. They are more objective than hand-drawn support and resistance lines or trend lines. In my experience, trades that have their setup near a cluster of Fibonacci support or resistance levels have a higher winning percentage.

It is well beyond the scope of this book to discuss Fibonacci at the level of detail it deserves.

Fortunately, as a thank you for buying this book, I am offering you a discount on my "The Fibs Never Lie" online video training course. This video course will teach you exactly how to implement Fibonacci into your own trading to increase your edge. Simply go to https://taooftrading.com/bookbonus to secure your training!

CHAPTER 7

BUY HERE, NOT THERE!

"Regression to the mean is the most powerful law in financial physics."

—JASON ZWEIG

If I was only allowed to use one indicator on my charts, it would be the 21 EMA.

The 21 EMA represents the "mean" or average price level of the stock over the past month (there are approximately 21 trading days per month).

At this point, I want to introduce you to a very important concept in trading called *mean reversion.*

It's such a powerful concept in trading, because the price of a financial instrument always mean reverts. Always, always, always.*

---

* The exceptions are if the stock goes bankrupt or gets taken over.

Consider these quotes from John C. Bogle, the founder of Vanguard Group:

"Reversion to the mean is the iron rule of the financial markets."

"It is very difficult for any particular segment of the stock market to sustain superior performance. The watch word for our financial markets is, 'reversion to the mean' i.e., what goes up must come down, and it's true more often than you can imagine."

That is to say, if price moves a long way away from its mean (which for our purposes is the 21 EMA), or spends a long time away from its mean, it is going to come back and find its mean (the 21 EMA) at some point.

Imagine there's an invisible elastic band that joins a stock price to its mean and you'll get the idea. Price can only get so far away from its 21 EMA before the elastic band becomes too stretched and pulls price back to the mean.

Let's have a look at this on a chart, so you can see this principle at work.

The chart below shows Facebook stock (ticker: FB) with the 21 EMA. Study the price action on the left half of the chart. Notice how when Facebook is in a downtrend (price is making lower highs and lower lows and the 21 EMA is downward sloping), price:

1. Spends most of its time below the 21 EMA.
2. Occasionally price gets a long way below the 21 EMA.
3. Whenever price does get a long way below the 21 EMA, price

will rally and revert to the 21 EMA. This is *mean reversion* in action, in a downtrend!

Now study the right half of the chart. Notice how when Facebook is in an uptrend (price is making higher highs and higher lows and the 21 EMA is upward sloping):

1. Price spends most of its time above the 21 EMA.
2. Occasionally price gets a long way above its 21 EMA.
3. Whenever price does get a long way above the 21 EMA, price will pull back and revert to the 21 EMA. This is *mean reversion* in action, in an uptrend!

This chart of FB shows how whenever price gets "too far" above or below the 21 EMA, it will eventually find its way back to (revert to) the 21 EMA.

Let me share with you some important lessons in trading that I have learned the hard way. Internalizing these lessons now could literally save you years of trading heartache that I wish I hadn't had to go through!

1. If a stock is in an uptrend, buying call options when the stock is near its mean is often a good idea.
2. If a stock is in an uptrend, buying call options when the stock is a long way above its mean is often a **less** good idea!
3. If a stock is in a downtrend, buying put options when the stock is near its mean is often a good idea.
4. If the stock is in a downtrend, buying put options when the stock is a long way below its mean is often a **less** good idea!

Let's keep this lesson simple. Here are two key guidelines I always recommend when trading options:

Enter trades when the stock price is near its mean.

Exit trades when the stock price is far away from its mean.

In other words, buy calls when price dips down to the mean in an uptrend (buy the dip!). Buy puts when price rallies up to the mean in a downtrend (sell the rip!).

I have found that by sticking to these guidelines, I have greatly reduced my number of losing trades (and dumbass FOMO trading mistakes).

When you're buying a stock that has already moved a long way from its mean, you are invariably chasing a move that is already well underway. Chasing moves can work, but I find it to be an exhausting, stressful way of trading.

This is not to say there aren't perfectly valid trading setups based on buying breakouts, buying new highs, etc. In fact, the "Turtle

Traders" we talked about in chapter 2 followed a twenty-day break-out strategy. It's just that with breakout strategies, you tend to have a very small number of very big winners. Many of these types of "breakout" strategies lose 70 to 80 percent of their trades but can make five to ten times or more on each winning trade. So, while they can be profitable overall—it's emotionally exhausting!

Very few aspiring traders I have met possess the mental toughness or discipline to stick with a strategy where only 20 to 30 percent of their trades are winning.

Personally, I do not find this type of trading to be emotionally rewarding, even if it can be financially rewarding.

I prefer to ring the cash register little and often. I prefer to target gains of 20 percent to 100 percent per trade but win 65 percent to 75 percent of the time. This is the type of return profile that is possible with the mean reversion trading I teach.

With mean reversion trading you are never chasing. You are simply waiting for the market to take a breath and come back to its mean.

The fact that you aren't chasing helps to take a lot of the emotion and urgency out of placing a trade. It's much less exciting, patiently waiting for the market to take a breath rather than watching to see if a stock breaks out. And that's a very good thing, as it helps to keep much of the emotion out of your trading.

Here's my big tip: If you're chasing excitement, go get your motor-cycle license. Go skydiving. Take up kite surfing. Heck, you can go have an affair for all I care! Just please don't come to the financial markets looking for excitement. Chasing excitement in the markets is your one-way ticket to financial self-destruction.

HOW FAR IS "TOO FAR"?

We have talked about NOT entering (and potentially exiting) a trade once a stock price is "too far" away from its mean.

So now you should be wondering, how far is *too far*?

To answer this, I'm going to introduce you to another indicator—Keltner Channels.

Keltner Channels were invented by—and are named after—Chester Keltner in the 1960s. Keltner Channels plot a line—or band—above and below an exponential moving average. The distance of the upper and lower bands from the EMA is determined by a multiple of the stock's average true range (ATR).

ATR is a method of measuring a stock's volatility, or degree of variability in price.

Traditionally Keltner Channels are plotted 1.5 ATRs above and below a 20 period EMA (these are the default settings on many charting platforms).

Here is an example of how traditional Keltner Channels appear on a chart:

Default settings for Keltner Channels plotted on a chart of GOOGL.

Notice how when a stock is in an uptrend, it spends most of its time between the mid-line and the upper channel. Occasions when the stock price gets back to its mid-line (or below) often represent a good buying opportunity in an uptrend.

Conversely, when a stock is in a downtrend, it spends most of its time between the mid-line and the bottom channel. Rallies to the mid-line (or above) often represent good selling opportunities in a downtrend.

Now, we want to use Keltner Channels to help us assess:

1. Potential entry and exit targets
2. When mean reversion becomes likely

To use Keltner Channels in this manner, we plot three sets of Keltner Channels on our chart as follows:

Mean (for all three)	21 EMA (this is the mid-line)
1st set of Channels	+1 and -1 ATR around the mean
2nd set of Channels	+2 and -2 ATRs around the mean
3rd set of channels	+3 and -3 ATRs around the mean

This is how they look, plotted on the same chart:

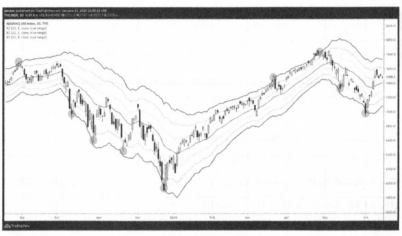

The shaded circles on this NDX chart highlight where the Keltner Channels tell us when price is "too far" from the mean and mean reversion is likely.

Here are the rules I apply for an uptrend:

1. A stock is in what I call the "action zone" when price is within +/- 1 ATR of the mean (i.e., near the mid-line). This is where we want to enter our trades.
2. When the stock price gets to 2 ATRs above the mean, this is a good, conservative profit target.
3. At 3 ATRs above the mean, it is more of a "stretch" profit target. Mean reversion (i.e., price falling back to the mid-line) becomes an increased probability at 3 ATRs above the mean.

The first question I always get when revealing these rules is: "So, does that mean I can short stocks when they are 3 ATRs above the mean?"

My response? It's always more difficult to make money by shorting (or buying puts on) stocks that are in an uptrend. That is the metaphorical equivalent of pointing your raft upstream on the Arkansas River. You can of course do whatever you like with your money, however shorting stocks that are trending upwards is going to be *hard work* (and has a higher probability of losing money).

Why?

Because when stocks are in an uptrend:

1. They are more likely to rise than fall.
2. Their upswings tend to be larger and go on for longer than their downswings.
3. Sometimes mean reversion occurs with the stock price trading sideways for a while, with the mean then rising to catch up with price (as opposed to price falling down to the mean).
4. Price can sometimes stay at 3 ATRs above their mean for a long time before they mean revert. Have a look at the chart of Citrix Systems below:

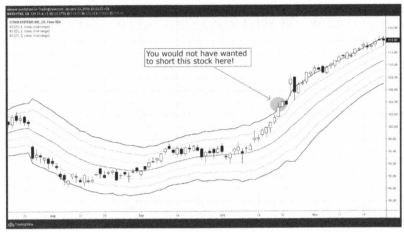

Don't be tempted to short a stock in an uptrend just because it is 3 ATRs above the mean!

The easiest way to make money trading stocks is to do this:

Trade bullish stocks in a bullish manner

Trade bearish stocks in a bearish manner

Bullish stocks are those that are in an uptrend. Look to buy calls in these to make money.

Bearish stocks are those that are in a downtrend. Look to buy puts in these to make money.

Humans love trying to pick the top in an uptrend or pick the bottom in a downtrend. Look, I get it. When we're contrarian, when we go against the herd, we feel clever. We feel like we've won against the odds and got a leg up on everybody else. We feel smarter than everyone else. Our ego *loves* this. But it is a difficult way to make money trading.

Stock market "experts" are always keen to tell us how "overvalued" the stock market is, or how "cheap" stock XYZ is, or how we should "buy when blood is running in the streets."

But honestly, buying stocks that are going up and selling stocks that are going down is the easy, low stress, high probability way of making money in the markets. Make sense? Good.

Before we finish this chapter, let's have a look at a couple more chart examples to witness the Keltner Channels in action.

The chart below shows Coca-Cola in an uptrend. Can you see how easy it is to go long (buy calls) when price is near the mean and sell when price is far away from the mean, using Keltner Channels?

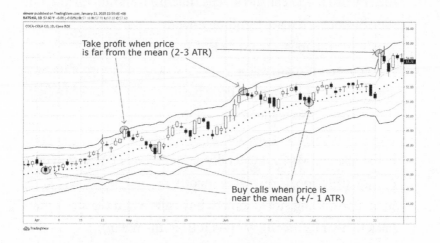

The chart below shows Tesla in a downtrend. Can you see how easy it is to short sell (buy puts) when price is near the mean and take profit when price is far away from the mean, using Keltner Channels?

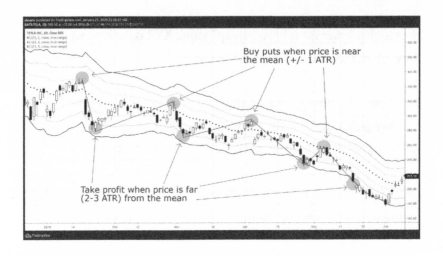

Buy puts when price is near the mean (+/- 1 ATR)

Take profit when price is far (2-3 ATR) from the mean

CHAPTER 7: PRO TIPS

- Trade bullish stocks bullishly and bearish stocks bearishly. In other words, buy calls in stocks that are trending up and buy puts in stocks that are trending down.
- We define the mean as the 21 EMA.
- When in an uptrend, a stock's price will spend most of its time above the 21 EMA, but will drop back to meet the 21 EMA from time to time (this is mean reversion).
- When in a downtrend, a stock's price will spend most of its time below the 21 EMA, but will rally to meet the 21 EMA from time to time (this, too, is mean reversion).
- In an uptrending stock, look to buy calls when the stock pulls back to near its mean (+/- 1 ATR from the mean).
- Look to exit when the stock is 2 to 3 ATRs above the mean.
- In a downtrending stock, look to buy puts when the stock rallies to near its mean (+/- 1 ATR from the mean).
- Look to exit when the stock is 2 to 3 ATRs below the mean.

Closing a position when price reaches 2 to 3 ATRs away from the mean is a great and simple strategy for setting profit targets. A more advanced way to set profit targets is to use Fibonacci extension targets. This is covered in my online video course "The Fibs Never Lie" which is available online. I am making this course available to owners of this book—for a massive discount. Please visit https://taooftrading.com/bookbonus to claim yours.

CHAPTER 8

WHY OPTIONS ARE YOUR BEST OPTION

"Options are like the Airbnb of the finance industry."

When somebody asks me to explain what an option is, I like to use the analogy of options being like the Airbnb of the finance industry (minus the annoying notifications that pop up on your phone about price rises in the area you just searched!).

With an option, you get the benefit of renting the stock (as opposed to the home) of your choice for a set period of time, without the significant cost associated with a purchase.

That's right, as option traders...**we don't make money from buying shares. We make money from *renting* them!**

Have you ever contemplated buying a Malibu beach house? How about a French Chateau in the Loire Valley?

It's a pipe dream for most us, isn't it?

But how about renting one for a week? Suddenly, doesn't this seem a whole lot more plausible and accessible? For a start, maybe you can actually afford to rent one for a week. Plus, you're not tying yourself down or overcommitting. Besides, you didn't want to *live* in the Loire Valley anyway...and pay for all the repairs and maintenance on some creaky old castle!

Options are similar, kind of. Instead of forking out $130,000 to buy 100 shares in Google (OK, I know they changed their name to Alphabet, but I stubbornly refuse to call them that), you can pay a fraction of that amount to "rent" Google stock for a set period of time.

Under the conventional "buy and hold" method of investing, you own a portfolio of stocks, ETFs, mutual funds, and bonds regardless of what the markets are doing. This means you are constantly exposed to market risk. Trump tweets, trade wars, recessions, bear markets, credit crises...yep, you are there for—and exposed to—all of that fun stuff!

You take in dividends (of 2 to 3 percent a year if you're lucky) and then you cross your fingers and rely on the fact that stock markets tend to go up, most of the time. At the end of the year, you are ecstatic if your portfolio earns you a return of 10 percent per annum because this is what Wall Street claims is a fantastic return.

As options traders, we are *far* more selective than "buy and hold" investors about our risk exposure. We choose to have exposure to risk only for brief periods of time, as opposed to all the time.

We are highly selective about when we choose to expose ourselves to stock market risk, too. We are always on the lookout for high probability moments in time to take any risk exposure.

As options traders we recognize that while stock markets go up most of the time, they can also chop sideways...and even fall! When stocks do enter a bear market, their prices can get cut in half (or worse). We don't want to passively sit through these potentially wealth-wrecking events feeling sick and scared. No, we want to actively participate and make as much money as possible when stocks are falling in price as well as rising.

THE APPEAL OF OPTIONS

If you want to trade the financial markets, there are many different instruments for you to choose from. The stock market is where most people seem to start, which is very understandable. Stocks are highly visible, they're always in the news, and we see them in our everyday lives. For example, brands like Apple, Microsoft, McDonald's, and Starbucks are all tradable on the stock market. We also hear about what the Dow Jones did on the news each night.

But there are many other choices of financial instruments for aspiring traders. Forex, futures, cryptocurrencies, and options are other common financial instruments that people will consider trading.

I have knowledge of and firsthand trading experience with them all, but the one instrument I always recommend and the one instrument that is always at the core of my trading is options. Stock options, to be precise.

When building a successful portfolio, every position you own should have the potential to positively move the value of your portfolio if it works well. You need to win big when you're right. But no position should be big enough that it could blow up your trading account if you are wrong. This is investment nirvana...and it is really difficult to achieve with stocks, forex, or futures.

Herein lies one of the key features of options trading: **Options offer limited downside and unlimited upside.**

Options offer great leverage for directional moves, up OR down (I'll explain exactly what this means later in this chapter).

And unlike forex or futures, you have a fixed amount of risk when buying an option. In other words, your account can't "go negative" as it can when trading forex, futures, or stocks on margin, when something crazy happens in the markets. If you're trading forex or futures and your account goes negative, you suddenly owe your broker money. The $5,000 you opened your trading account with could now be worth negative $2,000, for example. So not only has your initial balance been wiped out, you must transfer even more money into your broker just to square your account!

Futures and forex also offer decent leverage for directional moves, but in these markets leverage works both ways (i.e., for you when you're right and against you when you're wrong). Options are much easier to risk manage because they offer limited downside.

Additionally, options trades can be set up for an account of practically any size. Even if you're trading options in high-dollar value stocks like GOOGL or AMZN, an options trade can be set up that only costs a few hundred bucks.

With the massive rise in the popularity of exchange traded funds (ETFs), nowadays you can trade options on almost anything: individual stocks (e.g., Netflix, Coca-Cola, Mastercard); stock market sectors (e.g., technology, healthcare, financials); indices (e.g., the S&P 500, the Dow, the Russell 2000); interest rates (e.g., long-term treasuries, investment grade bonds, junk bonds); commodities (e.g., gold, oil, natural gas); and currencies (e.g., euro, Japanese yen, Aussie dollar).

Do you believe interest rates are going to rise? Instead of shorting bond futures and exposing yourself to unlimited downside risk, you can buy puts on a bond ETF (e.g., TLT). If you think gold prices are set to rise, you can buy call options on a gold ETF (e.g., GLD) instead of hoarding gold coins or bullion.

Options trading offers a world of fascination, because there are so many instruments and so many different ways you can trade them. A whole world of opportunity is just a few mouse clicks away.

Directional trading is when you believe the price of a stock (or any other financial instrument) is going to go up or down in a meaningful way. Buying an option is a great way to capture and potentially profit from these directional moves. And because there are so many instruments available to trade, you can nearly always find something with a strong directional bias that you would like to take advantage of.

ASYMMETRIC TRADING

This concept of unlimited upside with limited downside sounds almost too good to be true, doesn't it? But this type of trading even has a name—asymmetric trading. The word asymmetric might remind you of high school math, or triangles, or something.

But don't let the word asymmetric put you off...let it intrigue you!

Asymmetric simply means "not symmetric." As in, one side is different from the other. In the case of options, they offer an asymmetric payoff profile. This is because potential profits and potential losses are not symmetrical. Losses are limited (when compared with owning the underlying stock) while profits are unlimited.

This asymmetry is often illustrated by a payoff diagram, such as the payoff diagram for a call option below:

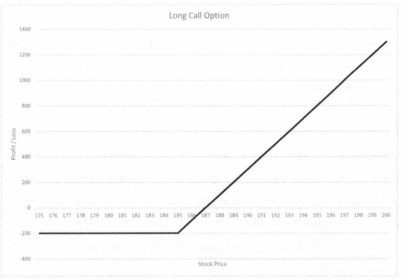

This payoff diagram shows the asymmetric nature of trading a call option—limited downside with unlimited upside.

Think of asymmetrical trading as the opportunity to make a significant profit from a small outlay. It is our job as traders to identify those moments in time when these asymmetric trading opportunities become a high probability, and that is what you are going to learn how to do in this book.

PRICE UP OR PRICE DOWN...WE CAN STILL MAKE MONEY!

The other fantastic—and really important—feature of options is they enable us to make money whether stocks are rising OR falling in price.

It's true that stock markets tend to go up most of the time. But when they do enter a bear market, the falls can be dramatic. We saw this happen both to the NADSAQ from 2000 to 2002 and to the S&P 500 from 2007 through 2009.

Bear markets like these can have a devastating effect on both the wealth and the psychology of traditional "buy-and-holders" who are praying for the market to go up every day.

As option traders, we lose this one-eyed view of the markets— always hoping that markets go up. Because we can make money whether stocks are rising OR falling, it is MUCH easier for us to remain emotionally detached from market action.

Instead of hoping and praying that the market always moves in a certain direction, we can instead remain genuinely curious about what happens next.

This emotional detachment from, and curiosity about markets leaves us in a very powerful place psychologically to make money from the markets. We are never relying on hope or blind faith. Instead we are relying on the skills and knowledge we have developed as traders, and we are putting those skills to good use in a practical and unemotional (and profitable) way.

SO, WHAT IS AN OPTION?

We are going to get just a little more technical in this section. It's necessary, for without learning the features (and the jargon!) of options, you won't gain a full appreciation for the wonder and versatility they offer. Neither will you understand what other options traders are talking about!

I want you to always keep in mind that an option is like a lease. It's like a rental agreement, but over a stock, rather than a car or a property.

FIRST, SOME DEFINITIONS

There are two types of options: Call options (calls) and put options (puts).

We buy calls when we expect the underlying stock price is going to go up. Just remember "call, up" (like call up a friend).

We buy put options when we expect the underlying stock price is going to go down. Remember "put, down" (as in, put down your shopping bag...you don't want to put down a friend).

So, we buy calls when we are bullish, and we buy puts when we are bearish.

All options have a strike price (also known as an exercise price and commonly referred to simply as strike) and an expiration date (I will sometimes refer to this as expiry date because it's easier to type).

When you buy a call, you pay what is called a premium upfront, and gain the *option* to *buy* 100 shares of the underlying stock, at the strike price, at any time from the day to buy the call, up until the option's expiry date.

When you buy a put, you pay a premium upfront and gain the *option* to *sell* 100 shares of the underlying stock, at the put strike price, at any time from the day you buy the put, up to its expiry date.

If a call option is like a lease agreement (you get to "rent" the stock for a set period of time), a put option is like an insurance policy (and you are paying "premium" to buy it). A put option's value will increase if the underlying stock price falls. In this way, put options are frequently bought to insure—or "hedge"—the value of an equity portfolio.

To reiterate, we buy calls when we are bullish on the stock (we think the price will rise) and we buy puts when we are bearish on the stock (we want to profit from an expected fall in the stock price).

Whenever you buy a call option, you are "long" that option. You have a long position in the call option. Being long a call option also means you are effectively long the stock, meaning you will profit when the stock price rises.

The terminology can get a little more confusing with put options. When you are "long" a put option, you will only profit if the stock price falls. So being "long" a put means you effectively have "short" exposure to the underlying stock. To avoid any confusion in this book, I will always refer to buying—or being long—calls, and buying—or being long—puts. If we are long calls, we expect the price to rise and if we are long puts, we expect the price to fall.

When we are long a call option (or options) on a stock (i.e., we have bought call options) this is called a "naked" long call position. A naked long put position is when we simply own a put option (or options) on a stock.

MONEYNESS

"Moneyness" (I double-checked and yes, this actually is a word!) is a term that options traders use when referring to whether an option is at-the-money, in-the-money, or out-of-the-money.

If you buy an option whose strike is closest to the current underlying stock price, the option is at-the-money (ATM).

For call options, when the strike price is above the current stock price, this option is out-of-the-money (OTM). These are the riskiest (and cheapest) types of call options to buy.

If the strike price is below the current stock price, the option is in-the-money (ITM). These are more expensive, but they have a higher probability of being profitable.

Have a look at figure 3.1 below which shows the options chain for Nike (NKE) options expiring on December 20, 2019.

Call option prices are on the left-hand side and put option prices are on the right.

NKE stock was trading at $89.18.

The at-the-money calls are the $90 calls, as these are the calls with a strike closest to the current stock price.

The easiest way to tell whether an option is in-the-money or out-of-the-money is to assess whether the option has any *immediate* value to the buyer of the option. If an option has immediate value, it is in-the-money. If an option only has potential value in the future, it is out-of-the-money.

Out-of-the-money calls are those with a strike higher than $90. There is no *immediate* value in an instrument that gives you the right to buy NKE stock at, say, $95 if NKE stock is trading at (or near) $90, right? So an NKE $95 call is out-of-the-money.

The in-the-money calls are those with a strike below $90. An instrument that gives you the right to buy NKE stock at, say, $85 when the stock is trading at $90 obviously has some *immediate* value. So an NKE $85 call is in-the-money.

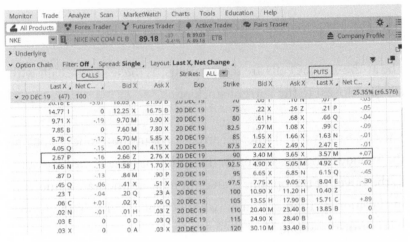

Figure 3.1—Options chain for Nike with at-the-money calls and puts highlighted.

With put options, they are also at-the-money when the put strike is the strike closest to the underlying stock price, the same as for call options.

Out-of-the-money puts have a strike price below the current stock price while in-the-money puts have a strike above the current stock price.

In figure 3.1, the at-the-money puts are also the $90 puts, as the $90 strike is closest to the current stock price of $89.18.

The out-of-the-money puts are those with a strike below $90. There is no *immediate* value in having an option that gives you the right to sell NKE stock at less than $90, when NKE is trading at (or near) $90. Therefore, the NKE $85 put is out-of-the-money.

Conversely, the in-the-money puts are all those with a strike above $90. If NKE is trading at (or near) $90, an instrument that gives you the option to sell NKE stock for, say, $95 obviously has some *immediate* value. An NKE $95 put therefore is in-the-money.

Here is a summary of what we have just discussed:

CALL OPTIONS

In-the-money	Call Strike < Stock Price
	We can buy lower
At-the-money	Call Strike = Stock Price (or closest to)
Out-of-the-money	Call Strike > Stock Price

PUT OPTIONS

In-the-money	Put Strike > Stock Price
	We can sell higher
At-the-money	Put Strike = Stock Price (or closest to)
Out-of-the-money	Put Strike < Stock Price

The easy way to identify the moneyness of an option is to remember that call options give us the right to buy the underlying stock. We would naturally want to buy at the lowest price possible, so calls with a strike below the stock price are in-the-money.

With put options we have a right to sell the underlying stock. We want to sell at the highest price possible, so puts with a strike above the stock price are in-the-money.

EXPIRATION

One of the key features that differentiates an option from a share is the fact that an option has an expiry date. A date upon which it literally ceases to exist.

Because options have an expiry date, they experience what is known as premium decay. Every day—all other factors being equal—

an option will lose a little bit of its value. That premium that you paid upfront will be worth slightly less tomorrow...and the next day, unless the underlying stock price moves in your favor. As an option gets closer to its expiry date, this premium decay accelerates.

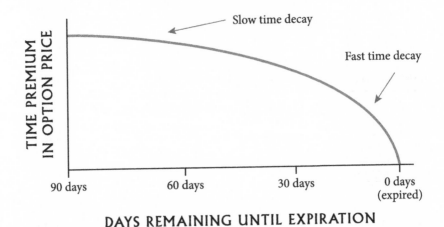

DAYS REMAINING UNTIL EXPIRATION

This diagram illustrates how premium decay accelerates as an option nears its expiration date.

This premium decay (also known as time decay, theta decay, negative theta) is the bane of options traders everywhere. It is the silent killer of failed options traders all over the world who were not equipped with the proper skills and knowledge before they commenced their trading journey. This book will equip you with the skills and knowledge necessary to ensure negative theta doesn't ruin your profitability as an options trader.

A Story That Illustrates Premium Decay

One of the many great things about living in Singapore is that you are only one flight away from almost anywhere in the world. But when that anywhere is New York, you've got to brace yourself for a long flight!

At eighteen and a half hours, Singapore Airlines flight SQ22 from Singapore to Newark is one of the longest commercial flights in the world. Spending more than eighteen hours inside a pressurized aluminum tube is enough to deplete even the most avid Netflix addict. In this story—in which you are the star—you've just been booked on this flight and you're not particularly looking forward to it.

So, imagine how pleased you are when, upon checking in at Changi Airport—Terminal 3, you learn that you have received a free upgrade to first class (those SQ first class suites are something to behold!).

After you board, you relax in your armchair while sipping on a glass of Billecart-Salmon champagne. Just before takeoff, an options trader who is seated down the back of the plane in economy, approaches you in your suite and whispers to you, "I'll pay you cash to swap seats with me. How much do you want?" You love your suite; you don't really want to leave it...but you are curious about how much money you could make on this transaction. He tells you he's willing to pay you $2,000 for the seat. You protest, pointing out that what he's offering is only 10 percent of the cost of the seat. He points out that you got it for free and asks again, "How much do you want for it?"

You tell him that you think $2,000 is too low, but if you get to sit there for the first five hours of the flight, he can have it for the remaining thirteen-and-a-half hours. You both shake hands on the deal.

Five hours later he heads back to your suite, ready to make the switch. He hands you $1,500 cash. "Hang on," you say, "we agreed to $2,000!" "Well yeah, but that was when we had an eighteen-and-a-half-hour flight in front of us. Now it's only thirteen-and-a-half hours. Time is running out." You tell him you want to think about it, and he walks off.

Three-and-a-half hours later he comes back to see if you've had enough time to think about it. "Sure, it's yours" you say, and he goes to hand you $1,000. "Whoa," you say, "we agreed on $1,500!"

"Yes, but now there's only ten hours left of the flight. Time is running out." You say you need to think about it again.

After a sumptuous dinner and a glass of fine Bordeaux, you pass out in your suite. You wake up feeling groggy, and groan inwardly as you see the options trader approaching your suite again. "Are you ready to switch seats yet?" he says, looking somewhat disheveled. He explains that there are now only four hours of the flight left. He may as well stay seated in economy but is still prepared to offer you $300 for your suite so he can get some work done in comfort before touchdown.

As you think about it, you realize that in four hours' time your seat will be worthless—this guy isn't going to pay you anything after the plane lands. So, you take the $300 and swap seats.

This is in illustration of premium decay in action on a long at-the-money call option. The closer you get to the end of the flight (the option expiration date) the lower the price you can get for your first-class suite (the option premium).

THE TWO COMPONENTS OF AN OPTION'S PREMIUM (PRICE)

Option premium is the price you pay for an option. It is comprised of two components, intrinsic value and extrinsic value:

Option Premium = Intrinsic Value + Extrinsic Value

Intrinsic value is what the option would be worth if it expired today. In other words, if all the time on the option suddenly disappeared, and it was exercised right now, how much money would you make? That's intrinsic value.

The first thing to note is that only in-the-money options have intrinsic value. In fact, "in-the-money" is literally another way of saying that an option has some intrinsic value.

The simplest way to think of extrinsic value is, it's everything else in an option's premium that is not intrinsic value!

Extrinsic value is also known as time value, and it can be thought of as the amount you're prepared to pay for an option in exchange for the benefit of controlling 100 shares for a set period of time.

Let's revisit the NKE options we looked at earlier in the chapter and work out what their intrinsic and extrinsic values are.

First off, let's look at the call and put options with the $90 strike and plug the prices into my intrinsic/extrinsic value calculator spreadsheet:

CALL OPTION		PUT OPTION	
Stock	NKE	Stock	NKE
Stock Price	$89.18	Stock Price	$89.18
Expiration	20-Dec	Expiration	20-Dec
Call Strike	$90.00	Put Strike	$90.00
Call Premium	$2.71	Put Premium	$3.53
Intrinsic Value	$ -	Intrinsic Value	$ 0.82
Extrinsic Value	$2.71	Extrinsic Value	$2.71

You can see that the call options have zero intrinsic value, which means they are either at-the-money or out-of-the-money.

You'll also notice that the put options actually have a small amount of intrinsic value, meaning they must be in-the-money. Strictly speaking, the $90 puts in this case are *slightly* in-the-money. But the option with the strike price that is closest to the underlying stock price is always considered to be the at-the-money strike.

Now let's look at the $85 strikes:

CALL OPTION		PUT OPTION	
Stock	NKE	Stock	NKE
Stock Price	$89.18	Stock Price	$89.18
Expiration	20-Dec	Expiration	20-Dec
Call Strike	$85.00	Put Strike	$85.00
Call Premium	$5.78	Put Premium	$1.66
Intrinsic Value	$4.18	Intrinsic Value	$ -
Extrinsic Value	$1.60	Extrinsic Value	$1.66

Here you can see the NKE $85 calls have intrinsic value of $4.18, which means they are in-the-money. The intrinsic value is simply the current share price of $89.18 minus the strike price of $85.

In the case of the NKE $85 puts, they are out-of-the-money, having zero intrinsic value.

If we look at the NKE $95 strikes, we can see that the calls are out-of-the-money (having zero intrinsic value) while the in-the-money puts have intrinsic value of $5.82.

CALL OPTION		PUT OPTION	
Stock	NKE	Stock	NKE
Stock Price	$89.18	Stock Price	$89.18
Expiration	20-Dec	Expiration	20-Dec
Call Strike	$95.00	Put Strike	$95.00
Call Premium	$0.87	Put Premium	$6.75
Intrinsic Value	$ -	Intrinsic Value	$ 5.82
Extrinsic Value	$0.87	Extrinsic Value	$0.93

(Note that for all the option prices in these examples, I am using the "mid" price, which is simply the average of the bid and ask prices.)

You can download this intrinsic vs. extrinsic value calculator spread-sheet for free at: https://taooftrading.com/bookbonus.

When we talk about premium decay, it is only the extrinsic value portion of an option's premium that is subject to premium decay. Extrinsic value converges to zero as the expiration date approaches. Extrinsic value will always be worth ZERO on the expiration date.

As a rule of thumb, an option will lose two-thirds of its value during the last third of its life. This is why buying very short-dated options is very difficult. The premium decay will most often get the better of you.

Intrinsic value only changes with changes in the underlying share price, and it is unaffected by the passage of time.

OPTIONS VALUATION 101

Intrinsic value we now know is very simple to calculate.

We know that only options that are in-the-money have it and we only need to do some first-grade arithmetic to calculate it.

Intrinsic Value (call option) = Stock price – call strike

Intrinsic value (put option) = Put strike – stock price

Extrinsic value is more complex to calculate. So much so, the developers of the first widely used options pricing model won the Nobel Prize in economics in 1997!

Don't worry, I am not going to take you down the rabbit hole of complex options pricing formula here. I just want to give you a general understanding of the inputs used to calculate the value of an option's extrinsic value.

An option's value has the following five inputs:

1. Underlying stock price
2. Implied volatility

3. Time to expiry
4. Dividends
5. Interest rates

Always remember, movement in the underlying stock price is king. It has by far the greatest influence over the price of an option, and it is the key thing we need to get right as directional options traders. If we buy a call, we want the stock to go up. If we buy a put, we want the stock to go down. But let's have a quick look at the other factors that impact an option's value.

Implied Volatility (usually referred to by the abbreviation IV) has the biggest influence over an option's extrinsic value, so let's cover this first.

IV tells us what the current price of an option implies about the expected size of future price movements of the underlying stock. It is a metric used to estimate the potential future fluctuations (i.e., volatility) of a stock's price. Greater implied volatility—that is, greater expected fluctuations in price—means the future path of the stock is expected to be more uncertain.

IV doesn't tell us whether a stock is going to rise or fall. It just tells us how much the market expects the stock's price to fluctuate in the future.

If the market has a view that the future fluctuations in the stock's price will be small, then the corresponding implied volatility (IV) will be lower. If the market has a view that the future price movements of the stock will be large, the IV will be higher. Rises and falls in IV are the main determinant of rises and falls in an option's extrinsic value.

If call options can be thought of as a lease, put options can be thought of as an insurance policy. When we think of them this way, we can see that when the future of a stock is more uncertain, there will be more demand for insurance on that stock. For example, eighteen-year-old male drivers are seen as more uncertain, more risky (more volatile?) than forty-year-old female drivers, hence their motor vehicle insurance premiums are more expensive. And so it is with stock option premiums. A stock's options will become more expensive if the market expects the stock price to be more uncertain, more volatile.

The key thing to remember is that IV is positively correlated with an option's value. A rise in IV will lead to a rise in the extrinsic value of calls and puts.

However, a rise in volatility is usually associated with falling stock markets/stock prices. That is, IV is usually inversely correlated with price. When price declines rapidly, IV tends to increase rapidly. For this reason, put options tend to do better than call options in environments of rising volatility. When stock prices fall, put options enjoy the double-whammy of an increase in intrinsic value (because the underlying stock price has fallen) and an increase in extrinsic value (coming from a surge higher in IV).

Under most circumstances, the price of the underlying stock is the dominant driver of an option's price. However during periods of extreme volatility, IV can become the dominant driver of an option's price.

Time to Expiry is also positively correlated with an option's value. The greater the time to expiry, the more expensive the option. If we go back to our "option as a rental agreement" analogy, this makes perfect sense. It will cost you more money to rent a house for two months than it will to rent it for two weeks.

Earlier in the chapter we discussed premium decay (also known as time decay or negative theta). This premium decay becomes more pronounced the closer an option gets to its expiry date. I rarely buy options with less than four weeks to expiry because premium decay is already becoming an issue at that point. I prefer to buy options with at least six to eight weeks of life left.

Dividends are basically a nonevent from our perspective. When a stock pays a dividend, its price generally falls by the amount of the dividend. A call option can become slightly less valuable after a dividend is paid and a put option becomes slightly more valuable.

Interest rates too, are really a nonevent for us. Rising interest rates will have a mildly positive impact on the value of call options and a mildly negative impact on the valuation of puts. The converse is also true, but in the real world this is not something we are going to try and trade as short term, directional options traders.

BREAKEVEN PRICE

It's important to know what the breakeven price of an option is at expiry. This can help give our strategy an important reality check.

Let's revisit the options chain for Nike options again.

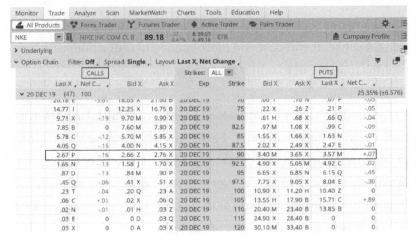

The option chain for NKE highlighting the at-the-money puts and calls with the $90 strike.

For a call option, the breakeven price is calculated the following way:

Breakeven Price (call) = Strike Price + Premium Paid

For example:

The NKE $85 calls have a breakeven of: $85 + $5.78 = $90.78

For these calls to be profitable at expiry, we need the NKE stock price to exceed $90.78. For a put option, breakeven is calculated thus:

Breakeven Price (put) = Strike Price – Premium Paid

For example:

The NKE $85 puts have a breakeven of: $85–$1.61 = $83.39

In other words, NKE stock would need to close below $83.39 for the puts to be profitable at expiration.

LEVERAGE

Earlier in the chapter I mentioned how options offered excellent leverage on directional moves. Now it's time to explain exactly what this term means.

First, let's define "directional move." A directional move is when a stock's price moves decisively in one direction or another. Such directional moves are quite common in trending stocks. This is why trend identification and analysis are important stepping-stones in becoming a successful options trader. You have already learned some simple yet highly effective techniques to identify trends in chapters 5 to 7 of this book.

Now let's explore the concept of leverage.

Remember, a call option is like a lease agreement over 100 shares.

So, when you buy a call option in Facebook, you get to "control" 100 shares of Facebook for a defined time period. You are effectively "renting" Facebook stock.

When you buy 100 shares in Facebook at today's prices (roughly $190 per share), it's going to cost you approximately $19,000. However, you can buy an at-the-money call option in Facebook that gives you control of 100 Facebook shares for 28 days, for just $550.

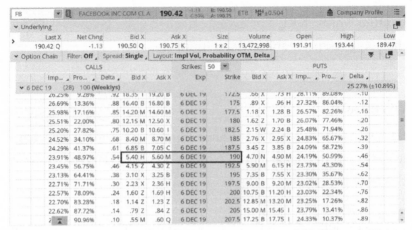

The mid price of FB at-the-money calls is $5.50, meaning you can control 100 FB shares for 28 days for a cost of $550.

Controlling the 100 shares of Facebook by buying an option costs you a mere fraction of what buying 100 shares of Facebook would cost you. But if Facebook goes up, you stand to make almost as much profit on the options as you would if you owned the shares.

This is what leverage means: large returns on a small capital outlay!

If the trade doesn't work out and Facebook shares fall, the most you can lose is what you paid upfront in option premium. You could obviously lose considerably more than this if you owned 100 shares of Facebook instead.

Have a look at the table below that shows the potential profit and loss of owning options versus shares of Facebook under scenarios of both rising and falling stock prices.

		Ticker	Stock Price	Strike Price	Premium	Intrinsic Value	Intrinsic Value %	Extrinsic Value	Extrinsic Value %	
		FB	190.42	190	5.50	$0.42	8%	$5.08	92%	
Outlay on stock purchase	$19,042.00									
Outlay on option purchase	$550.00									
% Change	40.0%	30.0%	20.0%	10.0%	5.0%	0.0%	-5.0%	-10.0%	-20.0%	-30.0%
Stock Price	$266.59	$247.55	$228.50	$209.46	$199.94	$190.42	$180.90	$171.38	$152.34	$133.29
Long Call Value at Expiry	$7,658.80	$5,754.60	$3,850.40	$1,946.20	$994.10	$42.00	$—	$—	$—	$—
Profit/Loss on Stock ($)	$7,616.80	$5,712.60	$3,808.40	$1,904.20	$952.10	$—	$(952.10)	$(1,904.20)	$(3,808.40)	$(5,712.60)
Profit/Loss on Stock (%)	40.0%	30.0%	20.0%	10.0%	5.0%	0.0%	-5.0%	-10.0%	-20.0%	-30.0%
Profit/Loss on Option ($)	$7,108.80	$5,204.60	$3,300.40	$1,396.20	$444.10	$(508.00)	$(550.00)	$(550.00)	$(550.00)	$(550.00)
Profit/Loss on Option (%)	1293%	946%	600%	254%	81%	-92%	-100%	-100%	-100%	-100%

Facebook (ticker: FB) stock is trading at $190.42. The $190 calls expiring in 28 days are trading at $5.50.

The cash outlay on the purchase of 100 FB shares is $19,042 while the cash outlay on the at-the-money call option is $550.

The table above shows how much money you could potentially make or lose on the stock purchase or the option purchase under various scenarios at option expiration.

For example, if FB stock was to rise 10 percent, you would make 10 percent on your purchase of 100 FB shares, or $1,904.20. You would however stand to make 254 percent on your at-the-money option if FB stock had risen 10 percent at expiry. If FB stock has risen 40 percent on the expiration day, you would stand to make 1,293 percent on your call options! Such is the power of leverage.

If FB stock falls 10 percent at expiration, you lose 10 percent on your 100 FB shares, or $1,904.20. Under this scenario you would lose 100 percent of the option premium you paid. However, you only paid $550 for the call option...and this is the maximum amount of money you can lose on the trade.

This is what I mean by my asymmetrical trading. If FB rallies 40 percent, you could make $7,108.80 on your option, but the most you can lose, ever, is $550. **Large potential returns on a small capital outlay!**

Let's go through some real-life examples that illustrate how leverage can be put to good use.

On February 19, 2019 I bought $115 calls in TWLO expiring on April 18, for $7.90. I sold them on March 13 at $15, for a **return of 89.9 percent in 22 days.**

A long call trade in TWLO.

On April 26, I bought $110 calls in TEAM expiring on June 21, at $5.25 ($525 per contract). I sold them on May 8 at $10.95 ($1,095 per contract) for a **return of 108.6 percent in 11 days.**

On July 1, I bought $115 calls in PYPL expiring on August 16, at $4.60 ($460 per contract). I sold them on July 11 at $7.88 ($788 per contract) for a **return of 71.3 percent in 10 days.**

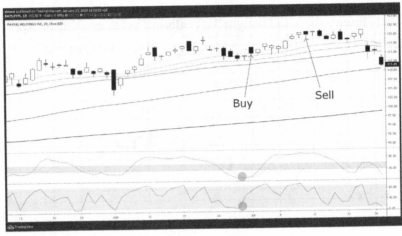

A long call trade in PYPL.

Are you beginning to appreciate the huge potential offered by trading options now?

UNDERSTANDING YOUR OPTIONS EXPOSURE

Now I want to introduce you to the fourth letter of the Greek alphabet...alpha, beta, gamma...**DELTA.**

Delta...I know, Greek letters and stuff...it all sounds a bit complicated. But much like *spanakopita*, it's really more straightforward than it sounds.

Options traders have created their own language over the decades, and it is necessary to learn some of these terms if you want to understand how options work. Again, don't be put off by any unfamiliar terms...allow yourself to be intrigued by them!

All options—both calls and puts—have a property known as a delta.

The delta on a call option is expressed as a positive number while the delta of a put option is expressed as a negative number. This is because put options move inversely with the stock price (i.e., put options go up in value when the stock price goes down, and vice versa). A call option's delta can range between 0 and 1 while the delta of a put option can range between 0 and -1.

Delta is an important concept because an option's delta can tell us many things about the option, and how it is likely to behave.

You might recall from your high school math or physics classes that the Greek symbol for delta (Δ) is used as an abbreviation for rate of change. Well, that is an important piece of information delta can tell us about an option, too.

First and foremost, delta tells us how much we can expect the price of an option to change in response to a fluctuation in the underlying stock price. Specifically, delta tells us theoretically how much an option's price will change given a $1 change in the underlying stock price.

For example, if a call option has a delta of 0.50 (often expressed as 50 delta, or delta 50), a $1.00 rise in the stock price would lead to a $0.50 rise in the option price. If a put option has a delta of -0.40, the value of the put will increase by $0.40 if the stock price falls by $1.00. These calculations aren't 100 percent precise but they are certainly close enough for our purposes.

The price of a call option with a delta of 1.0 will move one for one with the underlying stock price, while the price of an option with a delta of 0.01 will change in value by only $0.01 with a $1 change in the stock price.

Options with a delta of 0.50 (also expressed as 50) are at-the-money. Options with a delta of more than 50 are in-the-money and options with a delta less than 50 are (you guessed it!) out-of-the-money.

Options with a higher delta are more responsive to changes in the underlying stock price than options with a low delta. Options with a high delta are also more expensive than options with a low delta.

Have a look at the options chain for Facebook below and note how options with higher deltas also have higher prices.

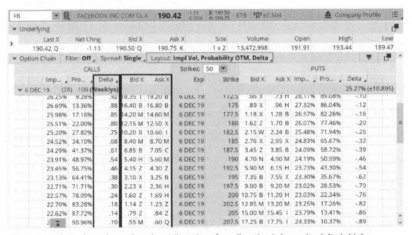

The options chain shows how when the strike price of a call option is lower, its delta is higher. Options with a higher delta are deeper in-the-money.

Another way to think of delta is in terms of the equivalent number of underlying shares we control. For example, if we own a call with a delta of 0.60, we are effectively long 60 shares. Even though an option contract covers 100 shares, our "delta adjusted" exposure is long 60 shares in this example.

If we own a put with a delta of -0.70, we are effectively short 70 shares.

Delta provides us with other insights too.

For example, delta provides us with the rough probability that an option will expire in-the-money. For example, a call option with a 0.50 delta has approximately a 50 percent chance of expiring in-the-money. A call option with a delta of 0.20 has roughly a 20 percent chance of expiring in-the-money.

This is important, as an option must be in-the-money at expiry to have any hope of being profitable at expiry. Remember that if an option is out-of-the-money at expiry, its value will be precisely zero!

By now, you are probably starting to see the appeal of buying in-the-money options. That is, options that have a higher delta. In-the-money options are attractive to buy because they are more likely to expire in-the-money. Yes, they are more expensive, but they also have a much higher probability of being profitable. Like most things in life, selecting the right delta option to buy is a balancing act. A balancing act we will discuss in detail in chapter 10.

KEY TAKEAWAYS

- A call option is like a lease agreement on 100 shares of the underlying stock. We get to "rent" 100 shares for a fixed period without ever actually having to own them.
- A put option is like an insurance policy on 100 shares of the underlying stock. We make money on the put option when the underlying stock price falls.
- Options provide us with the potential for massive profits for only a small initial outlay. This is called an asymmetric payoff and illustrates the power of leverage.

- We can make money with options whether stocks are rising OR falling by buying calls when we are bullish and puts when we are bearish.
- Buying calls and puts gives us the potential for unlimited upside, while our maximum downside is limited to the amount of premium we pay for an option.
- An option's price (called premium) is comprised of intrinsic value + extrinsic value. Extrinsic value of an option will always be worth zero at expiration.
- The delta of an option tells us:
  ◦ Whether the option is in-the-money (delta > 50), out-of-the-money (delta < 50), or at-the-money (delta ~ 50)
  ◦ How responsive the price of the option will be to changes in the underlying stock price
  ◦ The probability that the option will be in-the-money at expiration

THE FIVE KEY REASONS WHY WE TRADE OPTIONS:

1. Options offer us the best way to leverage a small amount of money into potentially significant returns.
2. Options enable us to be profitable in any kind of market condition.
3. Options offer unlimited upside together with limited downside, making it simple for us to manage risk.
4. Options can provide consistent opportunities for high probability trading.
5. Options are flexible and can be highly profitable in a stock market crash situation, when stocks, ETFs and mutual funds are all losing value rapidly.

CHAPTER 9

HIGH PROBABILITY TRADE SETUP FOR RAPID ACCOUNT GROWTH

In this chapter I'm going to share with you my favorite setup that I developed for trend continuation trades. This is the exact setup I use personally to catch moves with the dominant trend. I call these setups "Bounce 2.0" trades, as we are looking for price to literally "bounce" off a level of support or resistance within a trend. (The Bounce 2.0 setup is an improvement on an earlier "Bounce" setup I used in the past and has been tailored specially for short-term options trading.)

Imagine throwing a tennis ball on the ground. Our aim with the bullish Bounce 2.0 setup is to jump on that tennis ball as soon as possible after it hits the ground and starts bouncing back up.

Now imagine throwing a tennis ball at the ceiling. With a bearish

Bounce 2.0 setup, our aim is to jump on that tennis ball as soon as possible after it hits the ceiling and starts falling back to earth.

My objectives with the Bounce 2.0 setup are straightforward:

1. Determine the dominant trend of the stock we are considering
2. Locate a high probability moment in time to join that trend, with the expectation that the trend will continue

If we can identify a strong trend AND determine when the stock has mean-reverted to a level of support or resistance...BINGO! That is our high probability moment in time to join the trend!

A reminder that we are only looking at DAILY charts for this setup. I will occasionally look at smaller time frames when studying support and resistance. But for the purposes of these setups, we are only looking at—and taking trades from—the daily time frame (where one candle on the chart equals one trading day).

Before we jump into the specifics of the Bounce 2.0 trade, a quick review:

We want to see stacked EMAs to confirm a strong trend in either direction.

- For an uptrend: 8 EMA > 21 EMA > 34 EMA > 55 EMA > 89 EMA
- For a downtrend: 8 EMA < 21 EMA < 34 EMA < 55 EMA < 89 EMA

NB—when hunting for Bounce 2.0 trades, I use stacked EMAs for my scanning criteria (more on this in chapter 13), but on my charts,

I plot the following moving averages as I like to use the 50 SMA and 200 SMA as potential areas of support and resistance:

- 8 EMA
- 21 EMA
- 34 EMA
- 50 SMA
- 100 SMA
- 200 SMA

We want to enter a Bounce 2.0 trade (bullish or bearish) when the stock is in the "action zone" (i.e., within +/- 1 ATR of the mean, as we discussed in chapter 5).

There are two more indicators I want to share with you; I use them to help pinpoint Bounce 2.0 trades.

STOCHASTIC OSCILLATOR

The first indicator we are going to study is called the stochastic oscillator (also known as "stochastics"). Why is it called the stochastic oscillator? I honestly don't know. I guess its inventor, Dr. George Lane, liked the name! Anyway, the stochastic oscillator is a momentum indicator that shows the closing price of a stock in relation to its price range over a given period.

The stochastic oscillator is often cited as an overbought/oversold indicator. I don't like the terms "overbought" and "oversold" because they don't really mean anything.

Market commentators will often make the comment that a stock is overbought when they think its price is "too high." Too high relative to what? Usually just the commentator's own personal opinion, and you know what they say about opinions.

Similarly, people will comment that a stock looks oversold when they think its price is "too low." The terms overbought and oversold are loaded with subjectivity and I try to avoid using them.

Now, let me share with you the BIG problem associated with this line of overbought/oversold thinking. When a stock is in a strong uptrend, it can look overbought for a very, very long time. If you try to buy puts on a stock every time it looks overbought, you're going to have a thoroughly miserable time trading. Thus, the term overbought is virtually irrelevant.

The same is true for downtrends—a stock in a downtrend can look oversold for long periods of time. If you try to buy calls on a stock every time it looks oversold...well, you may as well just donate your trading account to charity rather than to people on the other side of your losing trades.

Have a look at the chart below and you'll see what I mean. SPY has been looking overbought for the past month according to stochastics, but price just kept on going up!

The shaded area shows SPY looking "overbought," but price continued to rally. Ignore "overbought" readings when a stock is in an uptrend.

Remember how even when a stock is in a strong trend, there is a natural ebb and flow to its movement? All stocks move in cycles.

The stochastic oscillator is not particularly useful in determining whether a stock is overbought or oversold, but it can be extremely useful in helping us determine where a stock is within its natural cycle of movement.

I use a Slow Stochastics indicator with a setting of 8,3 (or 8,3,3 on some charting platforms). I set the %K to 8 and the %D to 3. I set the overbought level at 60 and the oversold level at 40.

See the screenshots below for examples of how to set this up on some different charting platforms:

Stochastic Oscillator setup in Thinkorswim.

Stochastic Oscillator setup in TradingView.

Edit Stochastics 8 %K 3

Plot Style   Line ∨

Plot Color   ▢ ∨

Period   8 ⌃⌄

%K   3 ⌃⌄

Average Type   Simple ∨

Line Style   ———————— ∨

Line Width   ———————— ∨

Plot Opacity   ————————————————▮

Data Source   Price History ∨

Label

Leave blank for default

Ok

Stochastic Oscillator setup in TC2000.

The way I interpret the stochastic oscillator is as follows:

1. Assuming the stock is in a strong uptrend: a reading on the slow stochastic (8,3) of <= 40 means the stock has pulled back enough, within the context of its uptrend, to be considered for a bullish trade (buying a call). In a strong uptrend, there is a good probability that the stock will rise again (the uptrend will continue). This is a heads-up we can consider "buying the dip." I ignore any readings >60 in an uptrend; they are meaningless in this context.
2. Assuming the stock is in a downtrend: a reading on the slow stochastics (8,3) >= 60 means the stock has rallied enough, within the context of its downtrend, to be considered for a bearish trade (buying a put). In a strong downtrend, there is a good probability that the stock will resume falling again (it will continue its downtrend). This is a heads-up we can consider "selling the rip." I ignore any readings <40 in a downtrend, again they are meaningless in the context of a downtrend.

The stochastic oscillator gives us a good heads-up that the stock has just experienced a countertrend move that may be significant enough for us to consider a trade entry.

Let's see how this plays out on some charts.

In the chart below, Twilio is in a strong uptrend. The stochastic oscillator highlights potential buy-the-dip opportunities when the stochastics (%K) dips below 40 percent (see the shaded circles on the chart).

Stochastics highlighting potential buy-the-dip opportunities in TWLO.

In this chart, Nordstrom is in a strong downtrend. Stochastics (%K) highlights several potential sell-the-rip opportunities:

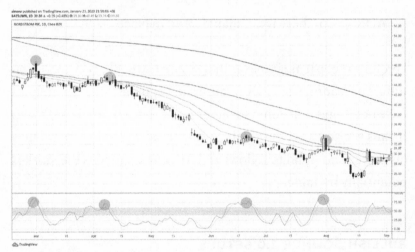

Stochastics highlighting potential sell-the-rip opportunities in JWN.

AVERAGE DIRECTIONAL INDEX

When the EMAs are "stacked," this is a great indication of a strong trend, but there is another indicator I like to use to confirm the strength of a trend. Let me introduce you to the Average Directional index, more commonly known by its abbreviation, ADX.

The ADX measures the strength of a trend. It doesn't tell us the direction of a trend, so looking at ADX doesn't give any insight as to whether the stock is going up or down. But it does give us insight into the *strength* of the trend.

The value of ADX can fluctuate between 1 and 100, with higher readings indicating a stronger trend. I use a 13 period ADX and this is how I interpret the readings:

ADX < 20 No trend, market is in chop mode

ADX >= 20 There is a tradable trend in place

I prefer to keep it as simple as that. Some textbooks will apportion different readings of ADX to different segments of a trend, but I have not found that doing so increases my edge. For me, ADX < 20 means the stock is not tradable using trend-following techniques (as there is no trend to follow) and ADX >= 20 means the stock *is* potentially tradable.

BULLISH BOUNCE 2.0 SETUPS

A bullish setup is one where:

- We have identified a stock that is in an uptrend
- There has been a short-term downtrend in price, i.e., a reversion to the mean

- We identify a trigger that indicates the stock is likely to resume its uptrend

For a bullish setup, we want to buy a call option in the expectation the price will continue to go up (remember "call-up").

Let's review the basic setup criteria for a bullish trend trade:

The stock is in an uptrend.

The EMAs are stacked in a bullish fashion:

8 EMA is above the 21 EMA

21 EMA is above the 34 EMA

34 EMA is above the 55 EMA

55 EMA is above the 89 EMA

The stock has had a pullback within the context of the uptrend.

Slow stochastics (8,3) <= 40

The trend is strong enough for us to expect it to continue.

ADX (13) >= 20

This simple set of criteria will help us identify stocks that are in a strong uptrend, but have pulled back enough within the context of the uptrend for us to consider buying a call option (buy-the-dip).

We also want to ensure that the stock is in the "entry zone," i.e., +/- 1 ATR of the mean (the 21 EMA). If the stock is in a very strong trend (i.e., ADX (13) > 35) a pullback to the 8 EMA is also acceptable.

The chart of PayPal below shows how this looks when it all comes together.

1. The EMAs are stacked
2. Price has pulled back to the 21 EMA
3. Stochastics (%K) has dipped below 40

Double-checking with the Keltner Channels, we can see that at point A, PayPal is within +/- 1 ATR of the mean, so this is all looking good so far!

A bullish Bounce 2.0 setup in PYPL.

Now all we need is an entry trigger to get us into the trade.

Just because a stock is in an uptrend and the stochastics have dropped below 40 doesn't mean the stock can't or won't keep falling. We need an additional signal to indicate that the pullback is most likely over, and the stock is likely to resume its upward path.

There are two entry triggers that I use for these setups. The first method uses another indicator, the Relative Strength Index (RSI), while in the second method, I study price action.

ENTRY TRIGGER #1—RSI ENTRY METHOD

Like the stochastic oscillator, the Relative Strength Index or RSI is a momentum indicator whose possible range is also bound in between 0 and 100. The calculation of RSI however is quite different from that of the stochastic oscillator. Rather than being concerned with whether price is closing in the upper or lower end of its recent trading range, RSI measures the speed and magnitude of recent price changes.

The conventional "textbook" way of using RSI is to use a 14-period RSI and interpret readings of >70 as "overbought" and <30 as "oversold." I have found no discernible edge in using the RSI this conventional way.

I use a 2-period RSI. A reading of below 10 on the 2-period RSI is quite uncommon in a strong uptrend and definitely gets my attention. When RSI(2) gets below 10 in a strong uptrend, it is an indication of a sharp pullback in price within the context of the uptrend.

What I'm looking for as an entry trigger is a situation where RSI(2) has dipped below 10 briefly, and then crosses back above 10. RSI(2) crossing back above the 10 level after having traded below 10 is a good indication that the sharp pullback is over, and the uptrend is likely to continue.

The only exception to this method is if the RSI(2) has been below 10 for more than four consecutive trading days. In my experience, when RSI(2) stays below 10 for five consecutive trading days or more, a more serious pullback is developing. A short-term rally may present after the RSI(2) crosses back above 10, but the risk of another leg down is much higher.

Most of the time in a strong uptrend, the RSI(2) will only fall below 10 occasionally and usually only for a day or two.

RSI(2) rising above 10 from below doesn't always nail the exact low of the pullback. Sometimes it is even a day or two early. But It usually gets us within spitting distance of the low, which more often than not, is close enough for us to make money.

Here's how the RSI(2) looks on a chart of Visa:

RSI(2) is on the bottom panel of this chart. The grey circles are entry bullish triggers highlighted by RSI(2).

You can see on the chart of Visa above, RSI(2) nails the low on three out of the four pullbacks but is early on the third one.

A more conservative way to use the RSI(2) entry method is to wait for RSI(2) to cross back above 10 and then study price action. What we are waiting for is for price to take out the high of the low candle.

In any pullback within an uptrend, there will be a price candle that marks the lowest point in the pullback we are studying. This is what I call the "low" candle. What we need to do for an entry trigger using this method is the following:

- Identify the "low" candle
- Identify the highest price of that low candle
- Wait for price to close above the high of the low candle

Let me show you what I mean using the price chart below:

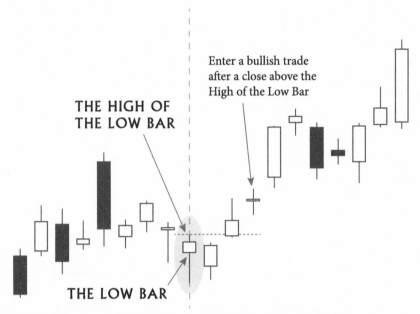

THE HIGH OF
THE LOW BAR

Enter a bullish trade
after a close above the
High of the Low Bar

THE LOW BAR

Wait for a close above the High of the Low Candle Bar before entering a bullish trade.

Now let's have a look at this on the PayPal chart. I have zoomed in on point A on the PayPal chart. The candle directly above the arrow is the low candle—the candle that has achieved the lowest price in the pullback.

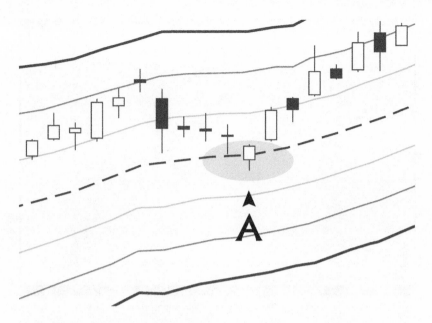

When price closes above the high price of the low candle, we can feel more confident that the pullback is over, and that price is now getting back on course to resume its uptrend.

When we get RSI(2) crossing back above 10, together with a close above the high of the low bar, this is an ideal entry trigger.

When it all comes together, we end up with a setup that looks like this:

The shaded circles highlight a "buy-the-dip" Bounce 2.0 trade opportunity in SBUX.

ENTRY TRIGGER #2–PRICE ACTION METHOD

We won't always get a pullback on the RSI(2) to below 10 in an uptrend. Quite often Stochastics (8,3,3) will drop below 40—indicating a tradable pullback—but we won't get an accompanying dip below 10 in the RSI(2). If we are only waiting for the RSI to get us into a trade, we will potentially miss out on some good trades.

The alternative entry method is to study price action once stochastics dip below 40 and wait for price to close above the high of the low bar.

By always waiting for price to take out the high of the low candle, we will always miss the exact low by a day or two. But it's worth it to avoid potential situations like this example below in Etsy. The shaded area in the chart below shows where price registers as a potential buy-the-dip opportunity according to the stochastics. By not entering the trade until we see a close above the high of the low candle, we avoid the potential of buying a stock that has further to fall. The low bar is the small, white candle after the succession of large, black candles. Waiting until we see a close above this low candle means we are buying a stock that has finished retracing, and is now more likely to resume its uptrend.

ESTY continues to fall after stochastics become oversold. By waiting for a close above the high of the low bar we greatly reduce our risk.

What we are looking for is this type of setup in NVDIA. We won't enter a trade just because we see our first oversold reading on stochastics. Instead, we'll wait until price closes above high of the low candle (the low candle is marked with the arrow).

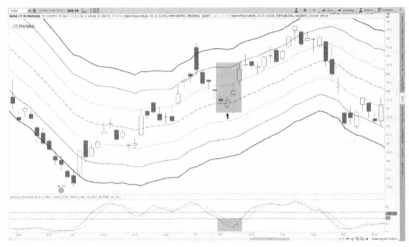

Price closing above the high of the low bar is our entry trigger in NVDA.

Once price starts moving in the direction of the dominant trend again, we can feel more confident that the pullback is over.

A WORD OF WARNING...

"Buy the dip" sounds great in theory. People always think, "Oh yeah, I'll buy the dip," but usually they don't buy the dip and often wait until the dip is truly over before they buy.

That's because "buy the dip" sounds great...until the dip actually comes. You see, dips rarely happen in a vacuum. Dips in price are often accompanied by some bad news or a scarier market environment. Buying the dip in practice is scarier in practice than it sounds in theory. So, when you identify a dip that can be bought using the Bounce trade setup, remember these things as per the Bounce 2.0 setup criteria:

1.   Stochastics are telling you the dip is relatively significant

2. RSI(2) and/or price action are telling you that the dip is potentially over
3. The trend is telling you that the path of least resistance is higher
4. You are buying off of a support level that should act as a price floor
5. These factors combined give you an *edge*

When the dip comes and everything lines up, have the courage to buy it.

BEARISH SETUPS

Bearish setups are really just the mirror image of bullish setups. However, I realize from having taught and mentored hundreds of students on how to trade, that making money from a falling stock price is less intuitive for most people. To make your life easier, I will provide step-by-step instructions for bearish setups here as well.

A bearish setup is one where:

- We have identified a stock that is in a downtrend
- There has been a short-term rally in price, i.e., a rally to the mean
- We identify a trigger that indicates the stock is likely to resume its downtrend

For a bearish setup, we want to buy a put option, in the expectation the price will continue to go down (remember "put-down").

Let's review the setup criteria for a bearish trend trade:

The stock is in a downtrend.

The EMAs are stacked in a bearish fashion:

- 8 EMA is below the 21 EMA
- 21 EMA is below the 34 EMA
- 34 EMA is below the 55 EMA
- 55 EMA is below the 89 EMA

The stock has had a pullback within the context of the downtrend.

Slow stochastics (8,3) >= 60

The trend is strong enough for us to expect it to continue.

ADX (13) >= 20

These criteria will identify stocks that are in a strong downtrend but that have rallied enough within the context of the downtrend for us to consider buying a put option (selling the rip).

We also want to ensure that the stock is in the "action zone," that is within +/- 1 ATR of the mean (21 EMA). If the stock is in a very strong trend (i.e., ADX > 35) a rally back to the 8 EMA is also acceptable.

This chart of AA highlights some "sell the rip" (put buying) opportunities in the downtrend.

As per the bullish setups, we need an entry trigger to get us into the trade.

Just because a stock is in a downtrend and the stochastics have risen above 60 doesn't mean the stock can't or won't keep rallying. We need an additional signal to indicate that the rally is most likely over, and the stock will start resuming its downward trajectory.

I use the same two entry triggers for bearish setups: RSI or price action.

ENTRY TRIGGER #1—RSI ENTRY METHOD

For a bearish setup, what I'm looking for as an entry trigger is a situation where RSI(2) has risen above 90 and then crosses back below 90. RSI(2) crossing back below the 90 level after having traded above 90 is a strong indication that the short-term rally is over.

The only exception to this method is if the RSI(2) has been above 90 for more than four consecutive days. In my experience, when RSI(2) stays above 90 for five days or more, there is an increased chance that a more serious rally is developing. A short-term drop may present after the RSI(2) crosses back below 90, but the likelihood of another leg higher is greater if RSI(2) has been over 90 for five or more trading days.

When a stock is in a strong downtrend, it is more likely the RSI(2) will only rise above 90 occasionally, and only for a day or two. These are the best signals.

RSI(2) falling below 90 from below doesn't always nail the exact high of the rally but it usually gets us very close, which most times is close enough to make money.

Ideally, we want the RSI(2) to fall back below 90 and for price to close below the low of the high candle.

When it all comes together, we end up with setups that looks like these in Philip Morris:

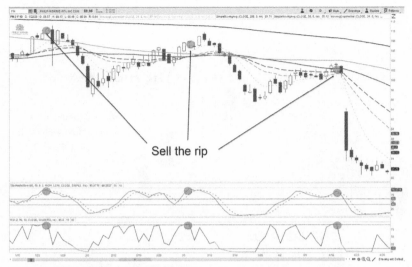

Sell the rip

RSI(2) entry triggers for bearish setups in MO.

Notice how in the second setup, the RSI(2) entry trigger would have got us into the trade a little early. In this example, waiting for price action to close below the low of the high candle would have provided a better entry.

ENTRY TRIGGER #2—PRICE ACTION METHOD

In any countertrend rally within a dominant downtrend, there will be a price candle that marks the highest point in the rally we are studying. Here's what we need to do for this entry trigger:

- Identify the high candle
- Identify the low price of that high candle

When price falls and closes below the lowest price of the high candle, we can feel more confident that the rally is over, and that price will resume its downtrend.

Please study the chart below for an illustration of this.

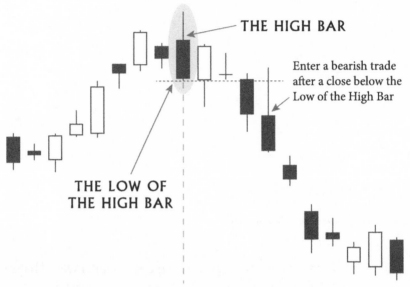

THE HIGH BAR

Enter a bearish trade
after a close below the
Low of the High Bar

THE LOW OF
THE HIGH BAR

We enter a bearish trade after a close below the low of the high candle.

Let's look at this on another chart. Here, I have zoomed in on a bearish opportunity in Alcoa. The high bar is highlighted by the shaded oval. We won't buy puts on this setup until after price has closed below the low of this high candle. We will enter the trade on the candle with the small black arrow above it, because the previous candle recorded the first close below the low of the high bar.

Notice that had we used the RSI(2) entry method on this particular setup, we would have gotten a better entry on the trade. Sometimes it works out this way, but using the price action method is generally the more conservative way to enter trades.

Wait until price has closed below the low of the high candle (highlighted) in this chart of AA.

Even though US stocks have been in a bull market for much of the past few years, there have still been some good bearish trading opportunities to exploit.

For example, on September 16, 2019 I bought $52.50 puts in CSCO expiring on October 18 at $3.10. On October 2, I sold these puts at $5.80, for a **return of 87.1 percent in 16 days.**

A bearish trade in CSCO.

CHAPTER 10

SETTING UP
THE TRADE

Once we have identified a potential setup, there are several other, more qualitative factors we should assess, in order to weed out the highest probability trading setups from the more marginal opportunities.

Here are the five criteria I analyze when confirming the setup (I refer to this as the "weeding out" process):

1. Is the setup near support (for a bullish trade) or resistance (for a bearish trade)?
2. Is the stock due to report earnings within the next two weeks?
3. Are there any very large gaps near the setup?
4. Are there any abnormally large candles near the setup?
5. Would this kind of setup have been profitable in the past?

Let's go through each one of these criteria in more detail.

IS THE SETUP NEAR SUPPORT OR RESISTANCE?

I always look to see if the setup I am considering is near a support or resistance level. Recall from chapter 6 that any the following can act as support or resistance:

- The 8 EMA, 21 EMA, or 34 EMA
- The 50 SMA or 200 SMA
- Horizontal support/resistance line
- Trend line
- Fibonacci retracements or extensions

I will generally pass on a setup unless price is at a support or resistance level. Remember, these are called "Bounce" trades. We want to see the stock price to be bouncing off something such as a support or resistance level. Things rarely bounce in midair!

When using EMAs as support/resistance, it always pays to study the "personality" of the stock in question. Some stocks in a very strong trend will frequently find support at the 8 EMA. Others may be more likely to pull back all the way to the 50 SMA before finding support. Eyeball the chart and see what it has tended to do in the past. If an uptrending stock usually pulls back to the 34 EMA before bouncing, don't expect the 8 EMA to act as a strong level of support.

If a stock has tested a level of horizontal support or resistance more than four times, remember that this level of support/resistance is likely to become *weaker* and the next test of that level may result in a breakout (in the case of resistance) or a breakdown (in the case of support).

Have a look at the chart of NKE below. Notice how the stock has found support at a price level that previously acted as resistance. This is an example of a resistance level changing roles and becoming a support level. Nike also found support at a round number ($90) and the 50 SMA. All these factors increase our edge on a potential long trade in Nike here.

Previous resistance becomes support in NKE.

IS THE STOCK DUE TO REPORT EARNINGS WITHIN THE NEXT TWO WEEKS?

US companies report earnings four times a year on a quarterly basis. Most companies report quarterly earnings mid-January to mid-February, then mid-April to mid-May, then mid-July to mid-August and finally mid-October to mid-November. Earnings announcements can have a significant impact on a stock's price. If a stock is due to make an earnings announcement within the next two weeks, I will generally pass on a Bounce 2.0 trade.

When an earnings announcement is near, it can cause the stock to trade in a less predictable manner. The problem is, as traders we have no way of knowing ahead of time whether a company is going to beat or miss earnings. And even if we did know that, we don't know how the market will react to the earnings result.

While some stocks will run into earnings, many don't. And the day of earnings can produce enormous volatility that is almost impossible to predict; 10 percent, 20 percent or even greater moves are possible on the day of earnings. Also, there is often little rhyme or reason to stock price moves on the day of earnings. Companies that supposedly "beat" earnings estimates can get sold off aggressively while other companies that supposedly "missed" earnings can rally. Of course, stocks can also get slammed when they miss earnings expectations and rally when they beat expectations. And sometimes, nothing much at all happens following the earnings announcement.

I very rarely hold options positions over earnings to avoid playing what I call "earnings roulette." To avoid getting caught up in a game of earnings roulette, always check whether the stock you are considering trading is due to report earnings over the next two weeks (ten trading days). If the stock is due to report earnings within that time frame, pass on the trade.

You can check for earnings announcement dates at http:// earningswhispers.com, http://barchart.com, and also on http:// tradingview.com charts.

There are other high probability trading setups that I use that specifically target pre- and post-earnings announcements. These are slightly more advanced techniques that are beyond the scope of this book. I teach them in my online options training course available at https://taooftrading.com.

ARE THERE ANY ABNORMALLY LARGE GAPS NEAR THE SETUP?

Gaps are areas on a price chart where no shares were traded within a particular price range. Normally gaps occur between the close on one day and the open on the next. There are two types of gaps: up gaps and down gaps. Up gaps develop as the result of extraordinary buying interest developing while the market is closed. Down gaps are the result of extraordinary selling interest developing while the market is closed.

Large gaps usually provide a good deal of price momentum in the same direction as the gap. I generally will not take a bullish trade if there is a recent large down gap in the stock. However bearish trades can work well after a large gap down.

Similarly, I will generally avoid taking a bearish trade if there is a recent large up gap in the stock. In this case I am going to be on the lookout for bullish trades.

How large is large? Just eyeball the chart. If the gap looks unusually large when looking at two years' worth of data, be cautious...especially if the gap is in the opposite direction of the trade you are considering.

There is (yet another!) old saying in technical analysis that "gaps get filled." It is more accurate to say that "gaps either get filled, or they don't."

It is true that small gaps within a strong trend tend to get filled quite quickly.

However *very large* gaps can often take a *very long time* to fill. Large gaps are usually the result of an earnings announcement that significantly beat or missed expectations, or some other type of announcement that surprised the market, either positively (in the case of an up gap) or negatively (for a down gap). Not only can large gaps take a long time to get filled, they can also act as a significant level of support or resistance.

Have a look at the Facebook chart below. The gap highlighted at A is a large gap down. We would not want to take a bullish setup against a down gap like this. Instead, we want to be stalking this stock for bearish trade opportunities after such a down gap.

The gap highlighted at B is also a large gap. Not as large as A, but still a large gap for the stock, and enough to reverse the previous bearish momentum. After an up gap like B, we want to be on the lookout for bullish setups. Also note how neither of these gaps have yet been filled, and gap A has been left unfilled for 18 months as of the time of writing.

Large, unfilled gaps on FB determine direction of price momentum for the next few months.

ARE THERE ANY ABNORMALLY LARGE CANDLES NEAR THE SETUP?

Very large candles indicate increased volatility. Increased volatility means increased uncertainty. Increased uncertainty means less predictability and therefore less edge in our setup.

I treat abnormally large candles as a warning sign. As with gaps, I am especially cautious if the large candles are in the opposite direction of the trade I'm considering. I will generally pass on bullish setups near abnormally large bearish candles and vice versa.

Have a look at the Wal-Mart chart below. That very large bearish (black) candle would cause me to pass on any potential bullish setup that may appear shortly after that candle.

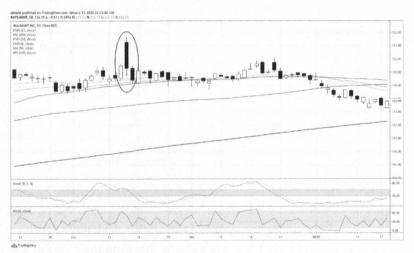

The abnormally large bearish candle on WMT (highlighted) is a red flag for any potential bullish setups that may follow in the near term.

HAS THIS SETUP WORKED IN THE PAST?

Before embarking on a trade, always eyeball the chart and look to see whether this setup would have resulted in profitable trades in the past.

The chart of Mastercard below shows that, of the last eight possible Bounce 2.0 setups this method has identified, seven of them would have been profitable. (I warned you there would be some losing trades!) Only setup number six would have resulted in a trade that didn't work out. I'm sure you'll agree that seven out of eight winning trades is a decent run-rate!

Seven of the last eight setups in MA would have worked out. Only setup number six didn't work.

Some stocks move in an erratic, volatile manner and don't trend well. These types of stocks may not play ball with trend continuation trades like this, so it is always worth checking the chart to see whether these setups seem to have worked in the past with the stock you are considering.

WHAT OPTION SHOULD I BUY?

By now, you understand that you want to buy a call option when you expect price to rise and a put option when you expect price to fall. The next decision we need to make is specifically which call or put should we buy for the trade in question?

Arriving at this decision involves answering two main questions, and they are:

- What expiration date do we want to buy?
- What strike price/delta option do we want to buy?

TIME TO EXPIRATION

I look to buy options with AT LEAST twice the amount of time to expiration as I expect to be in the trade.

For example, if I expect to be in a trade for two weeks, I want to buy an option with AT LEAST four weeks until expiration. It's always a good idea to buy yourself the luxury of time. I will often buy options with sixty to ninety days to expiration.

Have a look at the previous price swings on the chart. Approximately how long does the stock rally for, before making another short-term top? Is it one week, two weeks, or three weeks? Whatever the approximate average time period is, double it (at least) and that is how much time to expiration you want in the option you buy.

Generally, I'm not keen on buying a naked call or put with less than one month until expiry (earnings trades are one exception). I find the sweet spot to be two to three months in duration for this style of trading.

Many stocks have monthly and weekly options that trade. Monthly options expire on the third Friday of each month. Weekly options expire on the other Fridays of the month. It's always worth checking the volume and open interest on the options series you are considering buying.

Any good broker platform will have this information easily available in the options chain.

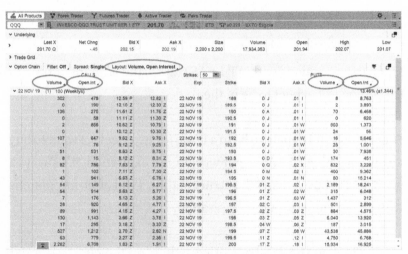

Volume and open interest for QQQ highlighted in the Thinkorswim options chain.

Volume refers to how many options were traded during the previous session. Open interest refers to how many options contracts are currently in existence for each option strike.

Monthly options tend to offer better liquidity, meaning a greater number of options are traded. This results in higher open interest and tighter bid/ask spreads (more on this later) than weekly options.

As a result, I usually prefer to buy monthly options over weekly options. Many stocks don't have weekly options available, in which case you have no choice but to trade monthly options.

Regarding open interest, I want to see existing open interest of *at least* ten times the number of option contracts I'm looking to buy. For example, if I'm considering buying three contracts, I want to see existing open interest of *at least* thirty contracts; more is better. I never want to be the only open interest in an option series. If the series is very thinly traded, I can expect a wider bid/ask spread when it comes time for me to sell my position.

IN-THE-MONEY? OUT-OF-THE-MONEY?

I nearly always buy in-the-money options for Bounce trades. Yes, they cost more than out-of-the money options, but like most things in life, you get what you pay for. The benefit of buying the more expensive in-the-money options is they have a much higher win rate.

In-the-money options have a higher win rate because:

- The breakeven price for an in-the-money option is lower. The underlying stock doesn't have to rally as much for us to make money.
- They have less extrinsic value. The impact of time decay is less pronounced on the value of in-the-money options.

When buying calls, an option with a delta of approximately 0.70 (or delta 70) is always my starting point. These options offer a good balance between the cost of the option and the amount of extrinsic value I must pay for the option. Sometimes I will buy options with a delta of 0.60, sometimes 0.80 (or higher) but 0.70 is always my initial go-to.

When buying puts, I'm happier to start with a delta 0.60 option because when we buy a put, we are expecting the stock price to fall. As you know from chapter 8, when stock prices fall, the implied volatility of the options nearly always shoots up. This increase in implied volatility helps to offset some of the time decay put options experience.

My other guideline for buying calls is I try to keep the extrinsic value down to roughly one-third of the total premium. For example, if the option premium is $3.00, I don't really want to pay more than $1.00 of extrinsic value if I can help it. For put options I am a little more lenient. In the case of puts, I want extrinsic value to be no more than 50 percent of the total option premium.

EXECUTING THE TRADE

Much like stocks you buy in the stock market, options have a bid/ ask spread (also known as bid/offer). The bid is the price at which market participants are prepared to buy, and the ask is the price at which market participants are prepared to sell.

For very liquid options, contracts like SPY (SPDR S&P 500 ETF), QQQ (PowerShares NASDAQ 100 ETF), and DIA (SPDR Dow Jones Industrial Average ETF), the bid/offer spreads tend to be very narrow—usually just a few cents. For most liquid, large capitalization stocks, the spreads tend to be quite manageable (10c to 20c). However, for less liquid stocks, bid/offer spreads can be quite wide. I have often traded options where the spread between bid and ask was wider than $1.00. Have a look at the options chains for the SPDR S&P 500 ETF and Fleetcor Technologies below.

					SPDR S&P500 ETF TRUST TR UNIT ETF **310.27**	-.50 -0.16%	B: 310.83 A: 310.87	ETB	±1.1	EXTO Eligible	

SPY

∨ Underlying

	Last X	Net Chng	Bid X	Ask X	Size	Volume	Open	High	Low
❯	310.27 P	-.50	310.83	310.87	1,500 x 1,500	54,664,690	310.89	311.01	309.39

∨ Option Chain   Filter: **Off**   Spread: **Single**   Layout: **Volume, Open Interest**

		CALLS			Strikes: 50 ▼		PUTS			
	Volume	Open.Int	Bid X	Ask X	Exp	Strike	Bid X	Ask X	Volume	Open.Int

∨ 20 DEC 19   (29)   100   13.82% (±9.712)

Volume	Open.Int	Bid X	Ask X	Exp	Strike	Bid X	Ask X	Volume	Open.Int
141	58,779	8.77 W	8.80 P	20 DEC 19	304	2.47 P	2.48 P	1,325	24,660
2,342	83,022	7.96 Z	7.98 W	20 DEC 19	305	2.69 P	2.71 P	17,667	204,402
620	46,501	7.16 Z	7.18 W	20 DEC 19	306	2.93 Z	2.95 P	5,619	19,050
542	35,488	6.38 P	6.41 P	20 DEC 19	307	3.20 P	3.22 P	3,562	29,835
52	544	6.00 Z	6.03 D	20 DEC 19	307.5	3.34 P	3.37 I	1,187	4,637
936	33,362	5.63 P	5.66 P	20 DEC 19	308	3.50 P	3.52 P	2,831	24,370
1,868	41,914	4.90 I	4.93 P	20 DEC 19	309	3.83 P	3.85 P	3,667	15,917
4,984	139,268	4.22 P	4.24 P	20 DEC 19	310	4.20 P	4.22 P	7,189	31,033
2,991	49,054	3.57	3.59 P	20 DEC 19	311	4.61 P	4.64 P	4,494	16,273
2,280	34,064	2.97 W	2.99 I	20 DEC 19	312	5.08 N	5.17 P	1,070	13,505
524	2,521	2.69 I	2.71 P	20 DEC 19	312.5	5.31 E	5.43 E	26	498
1,806	19,171	2.42 W	2.44 P	20 DEC 19	313	5.61 P	5.71 P	101	3,095
2,356	38,893	1.94 W	1.96 P	20 DEC 19	314	6.21 P	6.31 P	84	3,291
12,563	86,748	1.53 W	1.54 N	20 DEC 19	315	6.87 P	6.98 Q	11,973	11,824
76	33,390	1.18 W	1.19 I	20 DEC 19	316	7.59 P	7.71 Q	433	2,669

The bid/ask spread for SPY options is only $0.02 to $0.03.

					FLEETCOR TECHNOLOGIES INC COM **295.27**	-5.73 -1.90%	B: 245.06 A: 350.60				

FLT

∨ Underlying

	Last X	Net Chng	Bid X	Ask X	Size	Volume	Open	High	Low
❯	295.27 N	-5.73	245.06 K	350.60 K	1 x 0	465,201	300.59	301.88	294.575

∨ Option Chain   Filter: **Off**   Spread: **Single**   Layout: **Volume, Open Interest**

		CALLS			Strikes: 50 ▼		PUTS			
	Volume	Open.Int	Bid X	Ask X	Exp	Strike	Bid X	Ask X	Volume	Open.Int

∨ 20 DEC 19   (29)   100   24.09% (±16.128)

Volume	Open.Int	Bid X	Ask X	Exp	Strike	Bid X	Ask X	Volume	Open.Int
0	1	75.10 I	71.00 B	20 DEC 19	220	0 M	4.50 I	0	1
0	1	63.10 N	67.80 I	20 DEC 19	230	0 D	.85 C	0	1
0	1	53.70 I	58.30 I	20 DEC 19	240	0 A	4.90 C	0	2
0	1	43.60 A	48.20 B	20 DEC 19	250	0 N	1.50 M	0	20
0	15	34.10 P	38.50 I	20 DEC 19	260	.75 I	.95 M	2	120
0	4	26.20 M	27.80 M	20 DEC 19	270	.95 I	1.65 M	5	138
1	19	17.80 I	18.90 I	20 DEC 19	280	2.40 I	2.90 M	17	288
8	103	10.30 I	11.30 I	20 DEC 19	290	4.50 M	5.40 M	25	76
18	191	5.00 I	5.50 V	20 DEC 19	300	9.20 I	10.20 M	14	81
8	506	1.95 I	2.95 M	20 DEC 19	310	15.50 I	17.10 I	3	39
2	110	.55 M	.85 Q	20 DEC 19	320	23.10 P	27.30 A	0	2
0	1,159	.10 M	.55 M	20 DEC 19	330	32.50 I	37.30 A	0	1
0	10	0 E	4.90 C	20 DEC 19	340	42.60 I	47.40 B	0	1
0	1	0 E	4.90 C	20 DEC 19	350	52.70 B	57.50 M	0	1
0	1	0 E	4.90 C	20 DEC 19	360	62.70 T	67.50 M	0	1

The bid/ask spread for FLT options is $0.50 to $1.10.

Whenever buying (or selling) an option, always try to deal at "mid." Mid is simply the middle of the bid/ask spread. For example, if the bid/ask spread is $3.00/$3.30, mid will be $3.15.

This is less critical if the spread is only a few cents, but it becomes increasingly important as the spread widens. If the bid/ask spread is $0.30 or more, I'm quite particular about trading inside the spread.

For example, if the bid/ask spread is $5.20/$5.80, I will always work an order to buy at $5.50 initially. If that order doesn't get filled within five minutes, I will go for mid + 5c, i.e., if the stock price hasn't moved, I will increase my bid to $5.55. I will give the order another five minutes and if my order is still not filled, I will increase my bid to mid + 10c. If the spread is $1.00 or more and I can't get filled at mid + $0.15 I will just leave the order working and see what happens.

At this point, if my order does not get filled it's not a problem. I will either try again tomorrow if the setup is still valid, or simply flow to another opportunity.

SUMMARY OF THE BOUNCE 2.0 TRADE CRITERIA

1. Identify a strong trend:
   A. Stock is making higher highs and higher lows, or lower highs and lower lows
   B. EMAs are stacked
   C. ADX (13) >= 20
2. Look for a significant movement against the dominant trend (using stochastics)
3. Check that the setup is near support or resistance
4. Check for any abnormally large gaps or candles near the setup
5. Make sure the stock is not reporting earnings within the next two weeks
6. Look to see whether Bounce 2.0 trades would have been profitable on the stock in the past

7. Wait for an entry trigger:
   A. Price makes closes above the high of the low bar, or RSI(2) crosses above 10 (bullish trade)
   B. Price closes below the low of the high bar or RSI(2) crosses below 90 (bearish trade)
8. Buy an option with a delta of approximately 0.70 and with *at least* one month to expiry

CHAPTER 11

ADD SOME PEANUT BUTTER TO YOUR OPTIONS TRADING

Theta decay. Negative theta. Time decay. Premium decay. Four different names for the silent death of aspiring options traders. Call it what you like, this is the bane of directional options traders everywhere.

In this chapter, you are going to learn a straightforward options strategy that you can use to reduce or even eliminate the effects of negative theta. Think of it as a flu shot for your options trading!

I like to do what I can to minimize the effects of premium decay in my trading. Minimizing negative theta makes holding on to a position for longer easier, especially if the position has moved against you. Theta neutral positions are a lot more forgiving to trade and hang on to.

In fact, theta neutral directional options positions are pretty close to nirvana for an options trader because it is possible to get the best of both worlds. We get significant leverage to a move in the underlying stock, and we get the benefit of a small capital outlay and limited downside, but we get these features without experiencing the "death by a hundred cuts" of premium decay.

There are several different techniques options traders can employ to minimize the impact of negative theta on their options positions and their portfolio. Some of these techniques have funny names, like the butterfly, the diagonal, the iron condor, the jade lizard, and the rainbow unicorn. OK, I was joking with that last name. There's no such thing as unicorns. But all of the other names are legit!

Simplest is often the best in trading. The easiest setup for reducing or even eliminating the impact of negative theta from a directional options position is a simple strategy called the vertical debit spread.

WHAT IS A SPREAD?

Peanut butter? Nutella? Strawberry jam? Spreads can certainly make things more palatable, right? And the types of spreads I'm going to show you can certainly make holding an options position more palatable.

Once you have mastered the basics of buying call and put options, the next step in a trader's evolution is buying vertical debit spreads.

A spread is an options trade where we simultaneously buy and sell the same type of option with the same expiry date. It's just that the options that we are buying and selling have different strike prices.

We are going to use call debit spreads if we are bullish on the under-lying stock and put debit spreads if we are bearish.

A call debit spread is set up in the following manner:

- We buy a call option with strike price of X (we pay premium for this option)
- We simultaneously sell a call option with a strike price higher than X (and we receive premium for selling this option)

The call option we buy will always have a lower strike price and a higher delta than the call option we sell. To put this another way, the call option we sell will always have a lower delta and a higher strike price than the call we buy.

Trading debit spreads has some key advantages compared with trading naked call and put options and only one disadvantage.

The key advantages of debit spreads are:

- They are cheaper to implement
- They enable us to trade high share price stocks
- Trading spreads means we can take less risk
- Setting profit targets becomes super easy
- They reduce or remove the impact of premium decay

Their only disadvantage is that they cap our profit potential.

Let's look at each of these factors in more detail.

DEBIT SPREADS ARE CHEAPER TO IMPLEMENT

Because we are receiving premium on the sold option leg, the net cost of the trade is reduced, compared with a naked call option purchase.

Let's look at an example. Say we are bullish on Netflix (NFLX) We could buy an at-the-money $310 call expiring in two months for approximately $19.05 (which is roughly where the mid is). Remember, one option contract gives you control over 100 shares, so this option would cost $1,905 per contract.

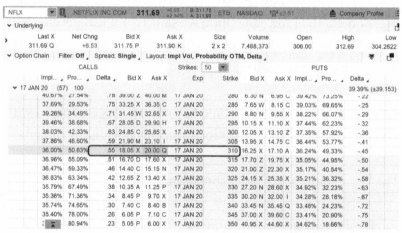

A NFLX 2-month $310 call would cost approximately $19.05 (bid/ask spread is $18.05/$20.00).

Alternatively, we could buy a $310/$320 call debit spread for approximately $4.25, or $425 per contract. This trade involves simultaneously buying a $310 call and selling a $320 call.

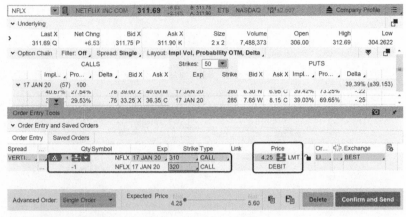

A NFLX 2-month $310/$320 call debit spread would cost $4.25.

By entering into a call debit spread, we are simultaneously paying premium for the long call ($310 strike) and receiving premium for the sold call ($320 strike). This reduces our net cost by $14.80, or $1,480 per contract.

DEBIT SPREADS ENABLE US TO TRADE HIGH SHARE PRICE STOCKS

Trying to trade a stock like GOOGL or AMZN (or NFLX!) with naked calls or puts requires quite a large account. You can see from the options chain below that a $1,700 call in AMZN would cost around $79.23 (or $7,923 per contract). But buying a $1,700/$1,710 call spread costs only $6.20 (or $620 per contract). So, by utilizing spreads, stocks with a high share price become tradable for traders with smaller accounts.

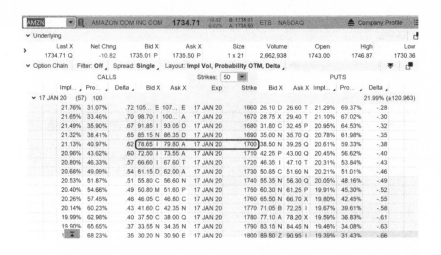

THEY ENABLE US TO TAKE LESS RISK

Because the cost to enter the trade is less, we are risking less money per contract on each trade.

SETTING PROFIT TARGETS BECOMES SUPER EASY

With a vertical debit spread, we always know what the maximum potential value of the spread is when we enter the trade. This takes all the stress out of setting profit targets.

The maximum value of a call debit spread is:

> Sold call strike (the higher strike price) – bought call strike (the lower strike price)

For example, if we have bought a $310/$320 call debit spread in NFLX, what we have done is:

> Bought a $310 call in NFLX

Sold a $320 call in NFLX

The maximum value of this spread at expiry is:

$320-$310 = $10

Since we know that we will never get more than $10 for the spread, we can set a sensible profit target. I target 80 percent to 85 percent of the maximum value of the spread for an at-the-money debit spread. So, if the maximum value of the spread is $10, I will work a sell order at $8 to $8.50.

DEBIT SPREADS REDUCE OR REMOVE THE IMPACT OF PREMIUM DECAY

This benefit is KEY. We can greatly reduce or even eliminate the effect of premium decay on our trade by buying a debit spread instead of a naked call option.

Let's look at the NFLX example again. The $310 call option we are going to buy as part of the spread has an extrinsic value of $17.28. Remember that this extrinsic value will be worth zero at expiration!

The $320 call option we are going to sell has an extrinsic value of $14.78. Selling this call option reduces the net extrinsic value we are going to pay to just $2.50 ($17.28 minus $14.78).

This *significantly* reduces the headwind of premium decay. Instead of $14.78 worth of option premium steadily decaying towards zero, we only have to contend with $2.50 worth of premium decaying to zero. This is a major advantage to trading vertical debit spreads.

| NFLX | ▼ | NETFLIX INC COM | **311.69** | +6.53 +2.14% | B. 311.75 A. 311.90 | NASDAQ | 184 +2.652 | ⏏ Company Profile |

Underlying

	Last X	Net Chng	Bid X	Ask X	Size	Volume	Open	High	Low
>	311.69 Q	+6.53	311.75 P	311.90 K	2 x 2	7,488,373	306.00	312.69	304.2622

Option Chain Filter: Off Spread: **Single** Layout: **Position, Intrinsic, Extrinsic**

			CALLS			Strikes: 50 ▼				PUTS			
	Posi...	Intri...	Extr...	Bid X	Ask X	Exp	Strike	Bid X	Ask X	Posi...	Intri...	Extr...	
												39.40% (±39.148)	
▼ 17 JAN 20	(56)	100											
	30.75	0.35 41.90 O	44.30 U		17 JAN 20	275	4.85 C	5.00 C	0	5.325			
	31.75	7.75	39.00 Z	40.00 M	17 JAN 20	280	6.30 N	6.95 C	0	6.625			
	26.75	8.05	33.25 X	36.35 C	17 JAN 20	285	7.65 W	8.15 C	0	7.90			
	21.75	10.30	31.45 W	32.65 X	17 JAN 20	290	8.80 N	9.55 X	0	9.175			
	16.75	12.225	28.05 D	29.90 H	17 JAN 20	295	10.15 X	11.10 X	0	10.625			
	11.75	13.60	24.85 C	25.85 X	17 JAN 20	300	12.05 X	13.10 Z	0	12.575			
	6.75	15.75	21.90 M	23.10 I	17 JAN 20	305	13.95 X	14.75 C	0	14.35			
	1.75	17.275	18.05 X	20.00 Q	17 JAN 20	310	16.25 X	17.10 A	0	16.675			
	0		17.15	16.70 D	17.60 X	17 JAN 20	315	17.70 Z	19.75 X	3.25	15.475		
	0	14.775	14.40 C	15.15 N	17 JAN 20	320	21.00 Z	22.30 X	8.25	13.40			
	0		13.025	12.65 Z	13.40 X	17 JAN 20	325	24.15 X	25.35 X	13.25	11.50		
	0		10.80	10.35 A	11.25 P	17 JAN 20	330	27.20 N	28.60 X	18.25	9.65		
	0		9.075	8.45 P	9.70 X	17 JAN 20	335	30.20 N	32.00 I	23.25	7.85		
	0		7.90	7.40 C	8.40 B	17 JAN 20	340	33.45 N	35.45 Q	28.25	6.20		
	0		6.575	6.05 P	7.10 C	17 JAN 20	345	37.00 X	39.60 C	33.25	5.05		

Buying a vertical debit spread can greatly reduce the amount of extrinsic value we have to pay, relative to a naked long option position.

If your brokerage platform doesn't show intrinsic value and extrinsic value of options in the chain, I supply an easy to use spreadsheet that will calculate this for you, that you can download for free in the bonus materials available at: https://taooftrading.com/bookbonus.

CALL OPTION		PUT OPTION	
Stock Ticker	NFLX	**Stock Ticker**	C
Stock Price	$311.69	**Stock Price**	$73.90
Option Series	17-Jan	**Option Series**	17-Jan
Call Strike	$310.00	**Put Strike**	$77.50
Call Premium	$18.97	**Put Premium**	$4.65
Intrinsic	$1.69	**Intrinsic Value**	$3.60
Extrinsic	$17.28	**Extrinsic Value**	$1.05
Extrinsic % of Premium	91%	**Extrinsic % of Premium**	23%

HOW TO SET UP A DEBIT SPREAD

There are a couple of different methods I commonly use to set up debit spreads. The first method is the one I use most often, and it involves buying an at-the-money option (delta of approximately 50) and selling an out-of-the-money option.

The second method involves buying a deeper in-the-money option (delta 70 or higher) and selling a less in-the-money or an at-the-money option (delta around 50 to 60).

Let's have a look at the characteristics of these two methods.

BUYING A DELTA 50 VERTICAL DEBIT SPREAD

This is a great strategy to use when:

1. We expect a strong directional move in the underlying stock
2. We want to reduce the impact of premium decay

Let's have a look at an example in Intel and assume we want to buy a call debit spread that expires in two months.

The first step is to locate a call with a delta of approximately 50.

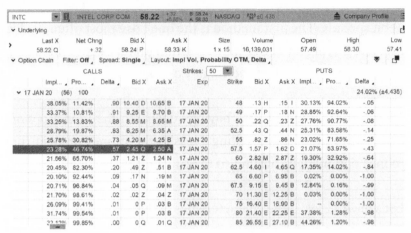

			CALLS			Strikes: 50				PUTS	
Impl...	Pro...	Delta	Bid X	Ask X	Exp	Strike	Bid X	Ask X	Impl...	Pro...	Delta
⌄ 17 JAN 20 (56) 100										24.02% (±4.435)	
38.05%	11.42%	.90	10.40 D	10.65 B	17 JAN 20	48	.13 H	.15 I	30.13%	94.02%	-.05
33.37%	10.81%	.91	9.25 E	9.70 B	17 JAN 20	49	.17 P	.18 N	28.85%	92.64%	-.06
33.25%	13.83%	.88	8.55 M	8.65 M	17 JAN 20	50	.22 Q	.23 Z	27.76%	90.77%	-.08
28.79%	19.87%	.83	6.25 M	6.35 A	17 JAN 20	52.5	.43 Q	.44 N	25.31%	83.58%	-.14
25.78%	30.82%	.73	4.20 M	4.25 B	17 JAN 20	55	.82 Z	.86 N	23.02%	71.65%	-.25
23.28%	46.74%	.57	2.45 Q	2.50 A	17 JAN 20	57.5	1.57 P	1.62 D	21.07%	53.97%	-.43
21.56%	65.70%	.37	1.21 Z	1.24 N	17 JAN 20	60	2.82 M	2.87 Z	19.30%	32.92%	-.64
20.45%	82.30%	.20	.49 Z	.51 B	17 JAN 20	62.5	4.60 I	4.65 Q	17.35%	14.02%	-.84
20.10%	92.44%	.09	.17 N	.19 M	17 JAN 20	65	6.60 P	6.95 B	0.02%	0.00%	-1.00
20.71%	96.84%	.04	.05 Q	.09 M	17 JAN 20	67.5	9.15 E	9.45 B	12.84%	0.16%	-.99
21.70%	98.61%	.02	.02 Z	.04 Z	17 JAN 20	70	11.30 E	12.25 B	0.03%	0.00%	-1.00
26.09%	99.41%	.01	0 P	.03 B	17 JAN 20	75	16.40 E	16.90 B	--	0.00%	-1.00
31.74%	99.54%	.01	0 P	.03 B	17 JAN 20	80	21.40 E	22.25 E	37.38%	1.28%	-.98
32.13%	99.85%	.00	0 Q	.01 Q	17 JAN 20	85	26.55 E	27.10 B	44.26%	1.20%	-.98

The INTC $57.5 calls have a delta of 57, which is the strike with a delta closest to 50.

The next step is look at the pricing of different spreads. What I am looking for is a spread where the cost of the spread is less than or equal to half of the maximum value of the spread.

For example, if I look at the INTC $57.5/$62.5 call debit spread, I know that the maximum value of this spread at expiration is $5. Therefore, the most I want to pay for this spread is $2.50. Even better if I can buy the spread for less than that!

We can see from the options chain that the $57.5/$62.5 call debit spread would cost approximately $1.98, which is below my threshold of $2.50.

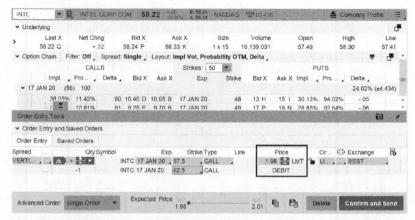

The options chain for INTC shows an indicative cost of $1.98 for a $57.5/$62.5 call debit spread expiring in approximately two months.

Let's have a look at the possible outcomes of this trade at expiration, using my call debit spread calculator.

	Ticker	Stock Price	Buy Strike	Buy Price	Sell Strike	Sell Price		Spread Cost
	INTC	$58.22	$57.50	$2.48	$62.50	$0.50		$1.98
% Change in Stock Price	15.0%	10.0%	7.5%	5.0%	0.0%	-5.0%	-7.5%	-10.0%
Stock Price	$66.95	$64.04	$62.59	$61.13	$58.22	$55.31	$53.85	$52.40
Long Call Value	$9.45	$6.54	$5.09	$3.63	$0.72	$—	$—	$—
Short Call Value	$(4.45)	$(1.54)	$(0.09)	$—	$—	$—	$—	$—
Spread Value	$5.00	$5.00	$5.00	$3.63	$0.72	$—	$—	$—
Profit/Loss	$3.02	$3.02	$3.02	$1.65	$(1.26)	$(1.98)	$(1.98)	$(1.98)
Profit/Loss %	153%	153%	153%	83%	-64%	-100%	-100%	-100%

This table shows a range of possible outcomes for a call debit spread in INTC.

You can see that with just a 5 percent rise in the stock price, the call debit spread would potentially achieve a gain of 83 percent.

With just a 7.5 percent rise in the stock price, the spread would potentially achieve a gain of 153 percent. This is the maximum return available for this call debit spread. Still, I'm sure you'll agree that a 153 percent return in two months (or less) is a decent return!

Of course, if the price of Intel has fallen at expiration, we could lose 100 percent of the premium paid. Let's compare this outcome with what would happen if we instead bought Intel stock.

Cost of the Call Debit Spread	$198
Cost of 100 Intel shares	$5,822

If Intel stock falls, the most we can ever lose on the call debit spread is the premium we paid upfront, i.e., $198.

So, if Intel stock falls 5 percent, we would lose $198 on the call debit spread, but we would lose $291.10 on the purchase of 100 shares.

If Intel stock falls 10 percent, we would still lose just $198 on the call debit spread, but we would lose $582.20 on the 100 shares.

This highlights again the other significant benefit of option trading...**limited downside**. No matter how far the stock price falls, the most you can lose in an option trade is the premium you paid upfront.

Risk management is still crucial though. I am going to do all I can to prevent an option trade from becoming a 100 percent loss. We will go over risk management in detail in the next chapter.

BUYING AN IN-THE-MONEY VERTICAL DEBIT SPREAD

This strategy is great to use when:

1. We are less bullish on the underlying stock, but we don't expect it to fall in price. In other words, we expect the stock to at least remain where it is.
2. We want to greatly reduce—or even eliminate completely—the effect of premium decay.
3. We seek exposure to a high share price stock whose options would be too expensive for our account size.

Let's assume we are slightly bullish on the price of Lululemon Athletica. At the very least, we don't expect the price to fall. Here's how we might structure an in-the-money call spread trade in LULU.

In this example, LULU stock closed at $219.90. We can buy a $200/$210 call debit spread expiring in approximately two months for $6.80.

In this transaction we are buying the $200 call and selling the $210 call, expiring in two months. Note that both the call we are buying AND the call we are selling as part of the spread are in-the-money. We are buying a spread that has a maximum value at expiration of $10, for $6.80 today.

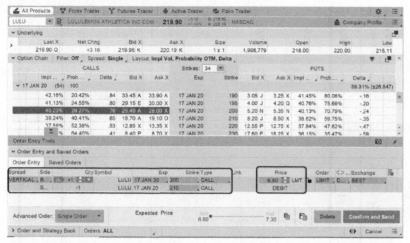

The options chain for LULU shows an indicative cost of $6.80 for the $200/$210 call debit spread expiring in approximately two months.

Looking at the call debit spread calculator below, you can see that the maximum potential return on this spread is 47 percent. This is what happens if the spread we paid $6.80 for is worth $10 at expiration.

The feature of this type of call debit spread—where both legs of the spread are in-the-money—is that we will realize the maximum return of 47 percent even if the stock doesn't move. In fact, the stock price can fall 5 percent and the spread will still make a 31 percent return!

	Ticker	Stock Price	Buy Strike	Buy Price	Sell Strike	Sell Price		Spread Cost
	LULU	$219.90	$200.00	$25.70	$210.00	$18.90		$6.80
% Change in Stock Price	15.0%	10.0%	7.5%	5.0%	0.0%	-5.0%	-7.5%	-10.0%
Stock Price	$252.89	$241.89	$236.39	$230.90	$219.90	$208.91	$203.41	$197.91
Long Call Value	$52.89	$41.89	$36.39	$30.90	$19.90	$8.91	$3.41	$—
Short Call Value	$(42.89)	$(31.89)	$(26.39)	$(20.90)	$(9.90)	$—	$—	$—
Spread Value	$10.00	$10.00	$10.00	$10.00	$10.00	$8.91	$3.41	$—
Profit/Loss	$3.20	$3.20	$3.20	$3.20	$3.20	$2.11	$(3.39)	$(6.80)
Profit/Loss %	47%	47%	47%	47%	47%	31%	-50%	-100%

This table shows a range of potential outcomes for an in-the-money call debit spread in LULU.

This is an extremely forgiving strategy because we don't even need the stock price to go up to make money. We just need it not to fall very much.

The other major benefit of this strategy is that it is virtually unaffected by negative theta. In fact, looking at the options chain below, you can see that the $200 call we are buying in this spread has extrinsic value of $5.75 while the $210 call we are selling has extrinsic value of $8.95. In other words, we are receiving more extrinsic value than we are paying!

Recall that at expiration, all extrinsic value is worth zero. So, the $5.75 of extrinsic value we bought in the $200 call will be worth zero, but so will the $8.95 of extrinsic value we received in the $210 call. In this transaction, we would receive net $3.20 worth of extrinsic value that will decay to zero by expiration.

What this means is that this call debit spread will actually benefit from time decay, as opposed to being its victim. This is yet another reason why this style of call debit spread is very forgiving.

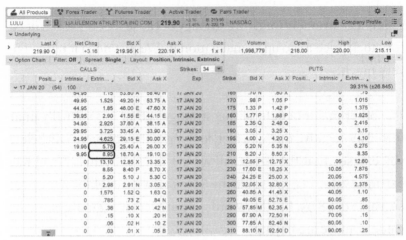

The options chain for LULU shows that the call option we are selling has more extrinsic value than the call option we are buying. The value of this spread will benefit from the passage of time.

The downside of the transaction in this example is that the maximum return on the trade is capped at 47 percent. But remember this trade has less than two months of duration and I'm sure you'll agree, 47 percent is still a handsome return.

The key benefits of an in-the-money call debit spread are:

1. The trade can still be profitable even if the stock price falls slightly.
2. The trade is largely unaffected by premium decay and may even be a beneficiary of it (as in this LULU example).

Here are a few examples of call debit spread trades I have taken recently.

On May 22, I bought a $197.5/$205 call debit spread in MCD expiring June 21, at $2.95 ($295 per contract). I subsequently sold the spread on June 7 at $5.50 ($550 per contract). I took a little heat on this trade, as the stock continued to pull back to the 34 EMA after

I entered the trade. In this instance, I would have been better off waiting for price to close above the high of the low bar. Still, the trade worked out well, **returning 86.4 percent in 16 days.**

On August 7, 2019 I bought a $150/$160 call debit spread in VRSK expiring September 20, at $3.95 ($395 per contract). On August 22, I sold the spread for $6.90 ($690 per contract) for a **return of 74.7 percent in 15 days.**

VERISK ANALYTICS INC, 1D, Close ROI

Sell Call Debit Spread

Buy Call Debit Spread

Created with TradingView

BUYING A PUT DEBIT SPREAD

We can also use put debit spreads to profit on falling stock prices.

For example, let's assume that we expect the price of Amazon stock to fall and look at an example of how we could structure a put debit spread in Amazon, to benefit from a fall in price.

Amazon stock is trading at $1,745.72. The $1,750 puts are closest to at-the-money.

The $1,750 puts expiring in approximately two months are trading at $53.55 (that is $5,355 per contract). We can sell the $1,740 puts with the same expiration for $48.85, with the resulting put debit spread costing $4.70 ($470 per contract).

Bought put option ($1,750 strike)	$53.55 paid
Sold put option ($1,740 strike)	$48.85 received

Net cost of spread	$4.70

The maximum value of the spread at expiration is:

Bought Put Strike – Sold Put Strike

$1,750–$1,740 = $10

For an at-the-money put debit spread, I want the cost of the spread to be less than or equal to 50 percent of the maximum value of the spread. In this example, the spread must cost less than $5 (which is 50 percent of the $10 maximum spread value). So the $4.70 cost qualifies.

We are paying $4.70 for a spread with a maximum potential value of $10. This means our maximum potential return is 113 percent.

The put debit spread calculator below shows a range of possible outcomes for this trade.

Ticker	Stock Price	Buy Strike	Buy Price	Sell Strike	Sell Price	Spread Cost
AMZN	$1,745.72	$1,750.00	$53.55	$1,740.00	$48.85	$4.70

% Change in Stock Price	7.5%	5.0%	2.5%	0.0%	-2.5%	-5.0%	-7.5%	-10.0%
Stock Price	$1,876.65	$1,833.01	$1,789.36	$1,745.72	$1,702.08	$1,658.43	$1,614.79	$1,571.15
Long Call Value	$—	$—	$—	$4.28	$47.92	$91.57	$135.21	$178.85
Short Call Value	$—	$—	$—	$—	$(37.92)	$(81.57)	$(125.21)	$(168.85)
Spread Value	$—	$—	$—	$4.28	$10.00	$10.00	$10.00	$10.00
Profit/Loss	$(4.70)	$(4.70)	$(4.70)	$(0.42)	$5.30	$5.30	$5.30	$5.30
Profit/Loss %	-100%	-100%	-100%	-9%	113%	113%	113%	113%

This table shows a range of potential outcomes for a put debit spread in AMZN.

If Amazon stock has fallen just -2.5 percent at expiration, the put debit spread will achieve its maximum potential return of 113 percent.

If Amazon stock remains exactly where it is at expiration, the spread will realize a loss of 9 percent.

If Amazon stock has rallied 2.5 percent at expiration the spread will be worth zero.

Here are a couple of real-life examples of put credit spread trades I have taken recently.

On May 7, I bought a $47.50/$45 put debit spread in WFC expiring June 21 at $1.00. On May 30, I sold the spread for $1.69 ($169 per contract) for a **return of 69 percent in 23 days.**

On May 23, 2019 I bought a $60/$55 put debit spread on COP expiring June 21 at $1.77 ($177 per contract). On June 5, I sold this spread at $2.75 ($275 per contract) for a **return of 55.3 percent in 13 days.**

This demonstrates how we can use debit spreads to profit on falling share prices. In the case of stocks like Google or Amazon, spreads are particularly relevant because buying naked put options in a high share price stock like these is quite expensive and therefore requires a large account.

I will cover risk management and position sizing in the next chapter.

PRO TIPS REGARDING DEBIT SPREADS

- We use call debit spreads when we are bullish and put debit spreads when we are bearish on the underlying stock.
- Debit spreads are a simple way to reduce or even eliminate the impact of time decay on our option trading.
- Spreads enable us to gain exposure to moves in an underlying stock while risking less capital, as they are cheaper to implement.
- The maximum value of the spread is known upfront which makes setting profit targets straightforward.
- Potential returns are capped when trading debit spreads.
- You can download the call debit spread and put debit spread calculators for free at https://taooftrading.com/bookbonus.

CHAPTER 12

YOUR KEY TO
TRADING SUCCESS

"Where you want to be is always in control, never wishing, always trading, and always, first and foremost, protecting your butt."

—PAUL TUDOR JONES

We've all experienced a parent, grandparent, teacher, or a boss who was good fun, quick to laugh, and great to joke around with. But every now and then, that person would get a look in their eyes or a tone in their voice that told you play time was over and it was time to pay attention. Well this chapter is the "it's time to pay attention!" chapter.

I understand that most of us get into trading "to make money." It's the reason I got interested in trading many years ago. But this very mindset—to make money—is the downfall of may aspiring traders.

Over the course of my career, I have had the privilege of meeting, working with, and befriending some of the best traders in the world, both clients and colleagues. They are people of different nationalities, different cultures, and different walks of life. But they all have one key trait in common. They are—without exception—excellent risk managers, first and foremost.

Risk management is the "secret sauce" that will preserve your trading account as well as your hopes and dreams as a trader.

Without proper attention to risk management, your failure as a trader is virtually guaranteed.

Let's start off by reviewing what risk actually is. Conventional financial theory confuses risk with volatility, or uncertainty. A key tenet of financial theory is that investments with higher risk also offer higher return. We have already debunked this nonsense in chapter 2.

Volatility is an important consideration for us as options traders, as we discussed in chapter 8, but it doesn't serve us well as a real-world definition of risk.

A better definition of risk is **the possibility of a permanent loss of capital**. Does that sound serious enough for you? Good. Risk management is a serious business!

Whenever you enter a trade, there is a probability that you will experience a permanent loss of capital as a result of that trade. It almost goes without saying that we must do what we can to manage and minimize this risk.

We can keep this risk to a minimum by:

1. Trading with a methodology that gives us an edge (you have learned just such a method in chapter 9). This way, over time, our winning trades will outnumber our losing trades.
2. Ensuring that our losing trades are small relative to our winning trades. We do this by mercilessly cutting trades that aren't working while letting winning trades run.

Here are some key truths in relation to trading and risk management that you must understand and come to grips with if you wish to be successful in this business:

- When trading, we are only ever dealing with probabilities, never certainties. Trading losses are inevitable. If this weren't so, trading would be a risk-free way of printing money and governments would have been made illegal a long time ago!
- When trading, we are only ever dealing with probabilities, never certainties. Even the best-looking trades can and do end up being losers (the same could be said for lovers, no?).
- A trading loss is not a failure or mistake. It is simply an operating expense. A cost of doing business. Any good business will do what it can to minimize expenses, but we can never hope to eradicate them completely.
- The market is not "out to get you." Never personalize trading losses. The market doesn't know or care that you exist.

"If you personalize losses, you can't trade."

—BRUCE KOVNER

Recall the following from chapter 3. As a professional trader, do you remember what your job is?

- It is NOT to be right
- It is NOT to predict the future
- It is NOT to pick tops and bottoms
- It is NOT to try and make money
- It is NOT to listen to financial media to try and stay on top of all the "news"

It's now time to explore these truths more thoroughly.

IT'S NOT MY JOB TO BE RIGHT?

Correct. I want you to GIVE UP on the idea of always wanting to be right. Successful traders excel at taking lots of SMALL losses and flowing from one opportunity to another.

This is a tough concept to grasp at first. Look, I never place a trade *expecting* it to be a loser. I wouldn't put the trade on in the first place if I didn't expect it to be a winner! But I know that every time I place a trade, anything is possible and there is always a chance that it will be a loser. I must accept this, otherwise I literally have no business trading in the first place. Assume that every trade you place is wrong until the market proves otherwise.

IT'S NOT MY JOB TO PREDICT THE FUTURE?

No. The future is unknowable. You must deal with the realities of the market in the here and now. Trade with an edge but always be open-minded to the possibility that ANYTHING can happen and plan your trades accordingly.

The market doesn't care how many lines of support you have drawn under your buy setup. The market doesn't care how convinced you are that a stock has finished retracing and is due to resume moving in the direction of its dominant trend. Even when trading with an edge, the market can and will do things that we don't expect. When you're in a position, constant vigilance and questioning is the order of the day.

Always remain genuinely curious about what is unfolding and open-minded about what could happen next. And never, ever trap yourself into thinking that the "market is wrong" just because it isn't conforming to what you initially expected.

When we impose our expectations on a trade, we ruin the trade. Expectations rob a trader of the ability to appreciate their current reality. For example, if you place a trade with the expectation it will book you a $2,000 profit, you may fail to appreciate the $700 profit that is there for the taking as the stock price unexpectedly starts moving in the opposite direction.

Expectations can cause us all significant stress when they don't line up with reality. This is as true in trading as it is in life.

IT'S NOT MY JOB TO PICK TOPS AND BOTTOMS?

That's right. You're getting the hang of this!

There is a crude saying in the industry that *"bottom pickers get smelly fingers."*

Picking tops and bottoms causes our ego to feel very clever, but it is a strategy that is fraught with danger. For example, to pick a bottom, you need to buy a stock that is still falling. This is very risky, as stocks that are trending lower have a strong tendency to keep moving lower. They have downward momentum.

Your job as a trader is to trade bullish stocks in a bullish fashion and trade bearish stocks in a bearish fashion. In other words, buy calls on stocks that are going up and buy puts on stocks that are going down. Stop trying to buy calls on stocks that are falling in price. Trade with the trend; it's so much easier.

IT'S NOT MY JOB TO TRY TO MAKE MONEY?

No, your job is to focus on the process. Enjoy the process and get really good at the process of trading, and the fruits of your efforts will manifest as trading profits (not orgasms!).

Avoid having any attachments to the outcome of each individual trade.

If you fixate on the outcome, you instantly start worrying, doubting, and mulling things that haven't even happened and may never happen.

Only take action because it's the right action to take because you're following a proven setup and you have your risk management rules in place. Know when you're going to enter the trade, know where you would like to take profits, and most important of all, know where your stop-loss is. Then, let the market do whatever the market is going to do...you have no influence over that anyway.

We want to avoid, at all costs, trying to impose our own convictions onto the markets. When we follow our convictions—rather than the evidence the market is presenting—we automatically filter out evidence that is contrary to our opinions. This is called confirmation bias and is something that anyone can easily fall victim to.

Having conviction in real life is a tremendous asset. It gives us drive, direction, persistence, and the staying power to achieve our goals. In trading, conviction is a major liability that can get us crushed.

"You can lose your opinion, or you can lose your money."

—ADAM GRIMES

"Losing a position is aggravating, whereas losing your nerve is devastating."

—ED SEYKOTA

IT'S NOT MY JOB TO LISTEN TO THE FINANCIAL MEDIA?

Absolutely not. The job of the self-serving financial media is not to inform, it is to attract clicks, draw viewers, and sell advertising. Its only job is to keep you glued to the screen so that you hang around to hear what they have to say, "after the break." The media's primary tools for keeping you addicted are fear and outrage. This is a massive distraction that will hamper—not help—your trading efforts. Please turn it off.

FORTUNATELY, YOUR JOB IS SIMPLE...

Your job as a trader is to manage the net liquidating value (NLV) of your trading account so that it grows consistently over time. That's it!

You're going to give up on the idea of always wanting to be right. You're going to stop worrying about being wrong or failing. You're going to divorce yourself from the idea that winning the next trade means you're a good trader.

INSTEAD, RISK MANAGEMENT WILL BE YOUR FOCUS

Never let a trade be so big or move so far against you that any of the following happen:

- Your focus shifts from looking for opportunities to trying to nurse a bad position back to health. The loss on any individual position should be small enough relative to your account size that cutting the position is an easy decision.
- You dread opening your brokerage platform for fear of what will be staring you in the face (large unrealized losses that you haven't been managing).
- You suffer guilt and regret (and sleepless nights) about a position that moved against you that you didn't do anything about.

Remember that crappy trades are stealing from you—stealing your time, money, and peace of mind. Show them no remorse and weed them out of your trading garden.

Now that you understand how critical risk management is to your trading success, you're probably itching to know how to do it.

I think of risk management in terms of two broad categories. They are:

1. Position risk: this deals with position size, and setting stop-loss and profit targets

2. Portfolio risk: this deals with portfolio diversification and hedging

All your trades should end in one of four ways:

1. A small win
2. A big win
3. A small loss
4. A scratch trade (breakeven)

Our aim as traders is to never experience a catastrophic loss. If you can just eliminate big losses from your trading, you have a great shot at being consistently profitable over the long term. This is what trading success looks like.

POSITION RISK MANAGEMENT

Managing position risk is how you manage the risk associated with each individual option position in your portfolio.

Every trading decision should have an exit strategy that is determined before you even enter the trade. Always have an answer to the questions: "How will I know if my idea isn't working?" and "What will I do if my idea doesn't work?"

Trading losses are inevitable. Fortunately, they are also completely survivable, provided you recognize them quickly and act to minimize their impact.

The key elements of position risk management are position size, stop-loss, and profit targets. Position size refers to what percentage of your NLV you allocate to each trade. Stop-loss is knowing when to exit the trade if things go wrong. Profit target is knowing when to exit the trade if things go right.

Let's look at each of these more closely.

POSITION SIZING

The conventional wisdom in trading is to only risk 1 to 2 percent of your portfolio in any one trade.

For example, say you have a $10,000 trading account, you would not risk more than $200 per trade using these guidelines.

This advice is sound, solid, and conservative. It is GREAT advice if you already have a large trading account. But if you have a small account that you are looking to grow, this advice will limit how quickly you can grow your account. It is the "safe but slow" on the freeway to financial independence.

Having a risk budget of only $100 to $200 per trade is also going to shrink the universe of potential trades you could consider.

If you have a smaller account (and by smaller account, I mean anything under $50,000), I advocate risking up to a maximum of 10 percent of your account per trade, under very specific circumstances.

"What? That's insane! No...it's reckless!!" is a common reaction to this way of thinking.

It's also an intellectually lazy response to this way of thinking—people allowing conventional wisdom to do the thinking for them.

Risking up to a maximum of 10 percent per trade is how I've traded and how I've taught hundreds of other people to trade. But it does require effort and a *rigorous understanding and implementation of risk and trade management.*

Let's continue to assume you have a $10,000 account size. Following this guideline, you now can risk a maximum of up to $1,000 per trade. In other words, your "risk budget" per trade is $1,000. However, when utilizing this position sizing method, I do not suggest allocating your entire risk budget to a trade all at once. You are placing too much pressure on yourself to time your entry with perfection. It's better to allocate 5 percent risk initially and then another 5 percent if the underlying stock reaches a predetermined milestone.

For example, maybe you have identified a good-looking bullish setup on a stock that has pulled back to its 21 EMA. But then you notice that roughly half of the time, the stock retraces all the way back to its 50 SMA on pullbacks. In this case, you have a couple of sensible choices you could make:

1. Buy a half-size position (5 percent risk) on the pullback to the 21 EMA. Then buy the second half of the position if the stock subsequently pulls back to the 50 SMA. The advantage of this method is the trade could start working straight away and you have exposure to the upside. The disadvantage is the value of any calls you bought on the initial retracement to the 21 EMA

could have lost quite a bit of value by the time the stock retraces to the 50 SMA.

2. Wait until the stock pulls back to the 50 SMA and buy a half-size position. Then buy the second half of the position when the trade starts moving in your favor (for example, when it crosses back above the 21 EMA). The advantage of this method is you get a great entry on the first half of your position and you are adding the second half of your position to a trade that is already working in your favor. This is always a great position to be in and **this is my preferred method of averaging into a position.** The disadvantage of this method is you may miss out on the trade altogether if the stock doesn't end up pulling back to the 50 SMA.

At this point, I implore you to NEVER worry about missing a trade. Ever! Trading opportunities literally pass us by like busses on a busy street, and there is ALWAYS another bus on the way! Sometimes we catch the bus that is in front of us and sometimes we must wait for the next one. In trading, there is ALWAYS another bus just around the corner. There is ALWAYS another pullback. There is ALWAYS another rally. There is ALWAYS another fantastic setup in the works that you can't see just yet. Don't ever feel afraid of missing out. Instead embrace JOMO—the joy of missing out!

If you miss a trade, never, never chase it. Just let go and focus on flowing to the next opportunity. Even if you thought it was the greatest setup in the world. The next "greatest setup in the world" is also just around the corner.

POSITION SIZE "SWEET SPOT"

"Risk no more than you can afford to lose, and also risk enough so that a win is meaningful. If there is no such amount, don't play."

—ED SEYKOTA

There is a subjective "sweet spot" that you will discover in your own trading.

If you are trading "too small," you will likely become bored. Neither the profits nor the losses will have any meaning for you, and you may start asking yourself, "what's the point?"

Bored traders are rarely profitable over time. Like a bored toddler, they get themselves into mischief by doing things they shouldn't, in an attempt to try to alleviate the boredom. They take marginal trades, ignore their trading plan, or start experimenting, or "tweaking" a perfectly good system. None of these actions are beneficial for their NLV.

A bored trader can also become apathetic towards their trading, without even being conscious of it. Apathy is bad because it leads to a lack of care with regards to entries, exits, and risk management. Bad trading habits can creep in under your awareness. And like any bad habit, once in place, they can be tricky to eradicate.

If you're trading "too big," you are going to be emotionally charged all of the time. You will be feeling surges of euphoria and fear with every swing in the market. One week you're feeling like a guru as you watch your NLV climb in value day after day. "I'm a genius!" you think to yourself, as you puff your chest out in pride. Until the market starts moving against you, as it inevitably will. Euphoria is replaced with fear, cold sweats, and feelings of uselessness and despondency.

This is bad. You are on the path to financial self-destruction if the emotional brain is running the show...as it surely will be if you are feeling surges of emotion with each swing of the market.

It is so important that you are able to recognize and be honest about your emotional state while trading. If you're feeling surges of powerful emotions (negative or positive), reduce your position size. If the possibility of losing 5 percent (or 10 percent) of your trading account in one trade freaks you out, trade smaller! Take less risk!

Always aim for emotional neutrality in your trading. Neither bored/apathetic nor euphoric/fearful.

If my emotions while trading venture anywhere beyond mild optimism to mild disappointment, I know I'm probably trading too big and may need to reduce the number of open positions I have on. (Either that, or I haven't meditated in a while!)

And whenever I feel as if I have got the market all figured out, I know it's just about to deal me a kick in the ass.

"Don't be a hero. Don't have an ego. Always question yourself and your ability. Don't ever feel that you are very good. The second you do, you are dead."

—PAUL TUDOR JONES

TRADE WITH MONEY YOU CAN AFFORD TO LOSE

With all the talk in this chapter about risk and the potential for losses, I'm going to endorse a piece of conventional wisdom that I agree with: *only trade with money you can afford to lose.*

If you are trading with money that, if lost, would adversely affect your lifestyle, you are placing far too much pressure on yourself to be immediately successful.

Nobody likes to lose money, but losing a small portion of your excess savings is going to have a very different emotional impact on you than losing next month's rent money. This is especially important when you are first learning to trade.

Make sure that any money you set aside for trading is not going to impact your ability to keep a roof over your head, food in your fridge, and clothes on your body.

If you're trading with money for which you have a future foreseeable need, your trading will be emotionally charged and stressful. This will only set you up for failure and broken dreams. You will be sweating every tick the market moves against you and nobody can expect to be successful under conditions of such stress.

You may aspire to become a full-time trader and make a living from trading. This is a noble and worthy goal, but the odds of you achieving this goal in your first few months of trading are slim indeed.

Imagine someone who aspires to make a living as a carpenter. They read a few carpentry books and dabble with some woodwork for a few weeks and then expect to successfully make a living in the trade. Does this sound realistic to you, or does it sound like a long shot? Chances are they'll need to put in the hours, get the proper training, and learn the craft properly if they really want to be successful in the trade. Trading is no different.

RISK BUDGET REDUX

We discussed above how, if you want to grow a small account aggressively, you will need to take more risk than the conventional "don't risk more than 1 to 2 percent of your account on any one trade" wisdom.

However, you still must not do anything ridiculous like risk half of your account on a trade.

In general, I won't risk more than 10 percent of my trading account on any one trade, and even if I do risk that much, I will do it in stages as outlined previously in this chapter.

If I have $10,000 and I want to buy calls in Apple, I could put up to $1,000 into that trade.

Does that mean I'm willing to risk $1,000 on my Apple trade and let those calls expire worthless?

Hell no!

If a trade is not working out the way I expect, I am NOT going to let it go to zero if I can possibly help it.

Which brings us to the discussion of stop-losses.

WHAT IS A STOP-LOSS?

Here's a personal story I want to share with you that illustrates how a stop-loss works.

THE LAP-DANCE THAT NEVER WAS

Back in September 2006, I was on a business trip in New York. My colleagues had taken me out for a fantastic steak dinner in Manhattan. It was late, we'd all had too much to eat and drink, so hitting a bar for yet another drink sounded like a perfectly good idea at the time. We jumped into a taxi (the iPhone hadn't been invented yet, much less Uber!) and hit a bar in the Lower East Side. It was a Thursday night. That Monday night I'd flown from Hong Kong to London, and Wednesday night I'd flown from London to New York. The jetlag combined with the evening's *filet mignon* and bottles of red wine got the better of me. I slumped in a booth while my colleagues had a drink at the bar. I drifted off into slumber.

The next thing I knew, I was being roughly shaken awake by a scantily clad young lady who was sitting on my lap.

"You owe me $200!" she shrieked at me.

"Huh? What? Who are you? What's going on? Get off me!" I stammered, groggy and still half asleep.

"You owe me $200! I danced for you! I gave you a lap dance and you owe me $200!"

"What?!" I protested. "I was just sitting here, minding my own business, fast asleep! You didn't dance for me. And even if you did, I missed the whole thing because I was sleeping! There's no way I'm paying you $200. Be on your way, there's a good lass," I offered.

"YOU OWE ME $200!!!!" she screamed.

I was starting to get a bit agitated, when a few seconds later, a bouncer appeared. A HUGE bouncer. This dude would have easily been 6'7" and 300 pounds. He put a massive hand on my shoulder and said to me sternly, in a deep baritone, "You owe the lady $200," while staring me straight in the eyes the whole time. He wasn't messing around.

I couldn't get the $200 out of my wallet fast enough!

Now, that $200 payment was my "stop-loss." I was happy enough to incur the $200 loss to avoid the possibility of incurring a potentially much bigger loss!

SETTING A STOP-LOSS

"If you can't take a small loss, sooner or later you will take the mother of all losses."

—ED SEYKOTA

In trading, a stop-loss is the level at which we want to get out of a trade because our idea didn't work out. The stock didn't move in the direction we expected or within the time frame we expected. We are happy enough to take a small loss, to avoid the possibility of incurring a much bigger loss.

When a trade doesn't work out as expected, we want to get out of it. Cut it. Close it out. We will take a small loss on the trade, and the reason we do this is to prevent a small, manageable loss from becoming a big loss.

If you want to stop a trade from going to zero, stop-losses are really important! This is particularly relevant for us options traders, given the premium decay that options experience. If a trade isn't going our way, we need to cut it mercilessly.

As you know by now, my default option to purchase is the delta 70. I like these in-the-money options as they decay less quickly than out-of-the-money options and their price is relatively less volatile when compared with cheaper, lower delta options.

My starting point for position risk management is to think in terms of a 50 percent "mental" stop-loss on my long options positions. For example, if I pay $3.50 for an Apple call option, I am almost always going to sell that call if the value of the option falls to $1.75 (i.e., 50 percent of the value I paid for it).

I call this a "mental" stop-loss because I almost never place a working stop-loss order with my broker. I watch the price of the option and if on a closing basis, its value is less than half what I paid for it, I will close the position the next day. I always make these decisions on a daily closing basis rather than intraday. Option values can swing about wildly during the trading day, but it is where the price closes that is important to me.

I don't like placing working orders for stop-losses with options because the price of options really can swing around a lot on an intraday basis. I don't want to needlessly get stopped-out of a good trade just because of some intraday noise. The one exception to this rule is if I have open trades and I'm going to be without internet access for an extended period (e.g., I'm trekking through the jungles of Myanmar or I'm on a transpacific flight).

If I'm buying low delta options (i.e., those options with a delta of 40 or less), I will risk the full amount of the premium paid and reduce my position size accordingly. I don't buy low-delta options often, but there are certain setups such as squeeze trades and pre-earnings trades where I will do this (I teach exactly how to identify, implement, and manage these types of trades in my option trading academy at https://taooftrading.com).

I will also look at the chart and follow price action in determining whether to stay with a trade. Remember that the most basic definition of an uptrend is a succession of higher highs and higher lows.

If I see a stock that was in an uptrend start making a lower low, the uptrend must be called into question.

Here is an example of what I mean.

In the chart below, Invitae has been making higher highs and higher lows, highlighted by the grey circles. If we are contemplating a bullish setup at point A, we should consider cutting the trade if price closes below point B. Why? Because if price closes below point B, it will have made a lower low. Price making a lower low, calls into the question the uptrend. It doesn't mean the uptrend is over. But it does mean something more complex, or something unexpected is happening and we are better off watching from the sidelines.

Point B in the NVTA chart would be a good place to set a stop-loss if we are considering a bullish entry at point A.

Let's now see what unfolded on the NVTA chart. Once we got a close below point B, which occurred at point C on the next chart, the uptrend was over. The trend flipped from up to down. By taking a small loss at point C, we avoided the potential of a far more significant loss that would have resulted if we had held onto the position.

Once the low at point B was taken out at point C, the uptrend was over, and the stock continued to make lower highs and lower lows.

SETTING A PROFIT TARGET

I showed in chapter 9 how, when using call debit spreads or put debit spreads, setting a profit target is very straightforward. For a delta 50 debit spread, I am typically looking for 80 percent to 85 percent of the maximum value of the spread as my profit target. For an in-the-money debit spread I will typically hold out for 95 percent to 100 percent of the maximum spread value as my profit target. If market conditions are particularly choppy or erratic, I may take profit on a debit spread position before this target is reached.

When buying naked long calls or long puts, selecting a profit target becomes a little more subjective.

While there are many ways of identifying a good profit target, I find the simplest methods are very often the best (as with most things in trading).

Let's revisit the chart with the Keltner Channels that we first encountered in chapter 7. Remember, we ideally want to enter Bounce 2.0 trades when price is close to the mean (the central line on the chart below, which is the 21 EMA).

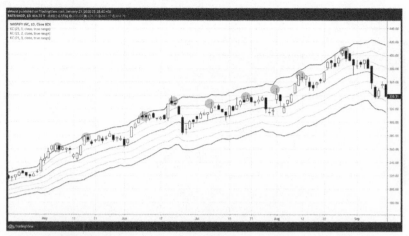

Two to three ATRs above the mean is often a good area to take profits. These areas have been highlighted on this SHOP chart.

For a stock that is in a strong uptrend, I want to enter the trade (buy calls) when the stock is trading close to its mean. I will generally take profit on at least part of my position when the stock reaches two ATRs (or more, depending on the strength of the trend) ABOVE the mean. Two ATRs above the mean is usually quite achievable for a stock that is in an uptrend. Three ATRs above the mean may be achievable for a stock that is in a particularly strong uptrend. It is always worth eyeballing the chart to see what levels the stock has a history of reaching during previous swings in price.

For a stock in a downtrend, similar guidelines apply. I want to enter the trade (buy puts) when the stock is trading near its mean. I will then look to take profit on the puts when the underlying stock is trading two ATRs (or more) BELOW its mean. Down moves in stocks tend to be swifter and sharper than up moves. If a stock is trending down strongly, it can often reach two ATRs below the mean quickly and three ATRs below the mean if it's in a very strong downtrend.

Two to three ATRs below the mean is often a good place to take profits on short trades.

PORTFOLIO RISK MANAGEMENT

When constructing a portfolio of options trades, I always want to ensure that I have a selection of different trades in my portfolio that are not all correlated to each other.

When different trades are highly correlated, they will have a tendency to all move up together at the same time and down together at the same time.

Imagine you have a lot of call options on technology stocks in your portfolio. You open your brokerage platform and see that your NLV is experiencing a nice increase on the day. You can pretty much guarantee that the NASDAQ is up that day, just by looking at your NLV. This is great, so long as the NASDAQ keeps rising. But what happens when the NASDAQ starts falling? Your NLV gets clobbered, that's what.

As we have discussed in previous chapters, options offer tremendous leverage. The magnitude of their price moves from day to day is much greater than the price moves you will see in stock prices.

This leverage—large potential profit for small capital outlay—is what offers option traders the potential for outsized gains. But it also means that the NLV of a portfolio of options trades has the potential to be highly volatile. It can swing around a lot if everything in the portfolio is correlated.

This is where diversification comes in. Diversification means having a selection of different trades that can move somewhat independently from each other.

I don't want a portfolio that is completely tied to the performance of the S&P 500 (or the NADSAQ, or any other index or market). The last position I want to find myself in, is hoping and praying every day that the market rises (or falls) each day in order for me to be able to make money.

Here are a few techniques I employ to try and ensure my portfolio NLV can grow smoothly over time, irrespective of what the market is doing.

FOCUS ON "RONIN" STOCKS

Many stocks are highly correlated with whatever the broader market is doing. They rise when the S&P 500 rises and they fall when the index falls. Their share price chart may even end up looking quite similar to that of the stock market index at times. There is no harm having one or two positions of these types of stocks in your portfolio. But my preference is to focus on stocks that are doing their own thing, without a care for what the broader market is doing.

I call these "Ronin stocks" after the Japanese term for a drifter or wanderer, a samurai without a master. Ronin stocks are those stocks that carve out their own path, stocks that are not beholden to a "master" (the market).

DIVERSIFICATION ACROSS INDUSTRIES

If I have $1,000 tied up in Intel in my $10,000 trading account, I still have $9,000 of "dry powder" to spend on other trades.

But if I put this money to work, it would not make sense for me to spend it on trades in AMD, Nvidia, Qualcomm, Micron Technology, Microchip Technology, and Texas Instruments.

I do not want to spend my whole risk budget—or even half of it—on semiconductor stocks. Sure, I could make a lot of money if semi stocks keep rallying, but my NLV is going to get absolutely pounded if the sector falls.

So, if I have a position in Intel, I am probably done as far as exposure to semiconductor stocks goes. I may add another technology stock (or two). Maybe a software company like Microsoft or Adobe. But 20 to 30 percent of my risk budget in technology stocks is probably as far as I want to go. After that, I will want to have some exposure to other sectors—healthcare, financials, consumer discretionary, consumer staples.

The chart below shows the weightings of the major sectors in the S&P 500. It is a good idea to spread your portfolio exposure across the major sectors and to be mindful of not overloading on any one sector.

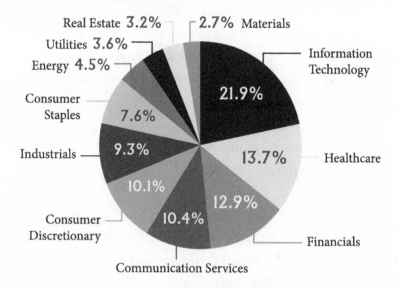

Real Estate 3.2%

2.7% Materials

Utilities 3.6%

Energy 4.5%

Information Technology

Consumer Staples

21.9%

7.6%

Industrials

9.3%

13.7%   Healthcare

10.1%

12.9%

Consumer Discretionary

10.4%

Financials

Communication Services

Based on GICS® sectors. The weightings for each sector of the index are rounded to the nearest tenth of a percent; therefore, the aggregate weights for the index may not equal 100%. As of Sept 30, 2019.

By being diversified across sectors, your positions in healthcare and consumer staples could potentially still be making money even if tech is going through a short-term rough patch, for example.

Let me share with you a nugget of truth I used to share with people on my team:

> If you don't have at least one position in your portfolio that is giving you the shits at any one time, you are probably not diversified enough.

DIVERSIFICATION ACROSS STRATEGIES

If you have exposure to a couple of market sensitive stocks, a few "Ronin stocks" and stocks from a range of different industries, you are off to a good start. But you also want diversification across different options strategies.

If you are 100 percent exposed to long call options, your NLV is going to suffer if the market experiences a sudden, significant drop. Heck, your NLV is most likely to suffer even if the market just chops sideways for the next few weeks!

You can mitigate this risk by making sure you have a mix of different options strategies in your portfolio.

For example, at any one time, I will usually have a combination of long calls, long call debit spreads, long puts, long put debit spreads, and maybe some call and put credit spreads as well. This way I am reducing how much negative impact my NLV will suffer from adverse market movements, while also limiting my exposure to the negative impact of premium decay.

When the stock market is trending, expect that approximately 75 percent of stocks will be moving in sympathy with the trend of the broader market. This makes perfect sense, as it is after all rising stock prices that cause the market to rise and falling stock prices that cause the market to fall.

But not ALL stocks rise in a rising market. In a bull market, we can expect approximately 75 percent of stocks will be in uptrends. That means approximately one stock out of every four will be in a downtrend. So even in a bull market, it's OK to have one or two bearish positions that can benefit from a fall in stock prices. This way, when the market pulls back (as it always does, the market never moves in a straight line forever), you'll have one or two positions in your portfolio that will benefit. This helps to smooth out the fluctuations in your portfolio NLV.

PORTFOLIO/NLV STOP-LOSS

We discussed earlier in this chapter how important it is to have a stop-loss on individual options positions and to cut without mercy any positions that are performing contrary to our expectations.

In addition to running stop-losses on my individual positions, I also run a stop-loss on my portfolio NLV. I do this by applying a trailing 15 percent "peak to trough" stop-loss on my NLV. If my NLV stop-loss is hit, I close all my open positions and go "flat" (i.e., 100 percent cash). I will then pause all trading for twenty-four hours while I CTFO (chill out) and recollect my thoughts.

It is mentally and psychologically refreshing to have a pause from trading, especially if you've been having a tough time in the market. Trading is not one of those pursuits in life where the harder you try, the better your results. In fact, the opposite is more likely to be true in trading. If I ever feel like I'm struggling or doing battle with the market from day to day, a short break from trading has worked wonders.

Increased "efforting" when you're going through a tough patch in trading will only tend to make things worse.

Here's an example of how this NLV stop-loss works: Say my account started at $10,000. A couple of months later after a few good trades, my portfolio hits a new high NLV of $15,000. My new "cut every position and go flat" stop-loss is activated if my NLV falls 15 percent from its peak; in this example, I will do this if my NLV falls to $12,750.

Part of my overriding objective when structuring my portfolio is ensuring this doesn't happen often. By being vigilant with regards to...

1. Only entering trades with the trend, where I have an edge
2. Correct position sizing
3. Managing stop-losses on individual positions
4. Ensuring proper diversification across industries (e.g., I'm not 50 percent weighted to financial stocks)
5. Ensuring my options strategies are diversified (e.g., my portfolio is not 100 percent long call options)

I'm doing everything I can to ensure that my portfolio NLV stop-loss is not hit very often.

I'm not enforcing the 15 percent from peak NLV stop-loss as a form of punishment on myself. I am enforcing it to ensure that I am always mindful of constructing and managing my portfolio in such a way as to minimize the probability of a sharp, negative move in my NLV. It helps to ensure consistency in my trading results. This discipline also has the benefit of ensuring that I take a refreshing pause from trading when I most need it.

HEDGING

Another important technique I use to minimize the risk to my NLV risk is hedging, a technique I will outline in this section.

Most of the time, markets trend up. At other times, markets can trend down. If the market is trending up, my portfolio is going to be comprised predominantly of bullish positions (e.g., long calls, long call debit spreads). If the market is trending down, my portfolio is going to be predominantly comprised of bearish positions (e.g., long puts, long put debit spreads).

Even in an uptrend, the market can go through periods of time when it falls (and vice versa). When trading short-term, leveraged instruments like options—even fairly small movements against the trend—can really hurt our NLV.

A hedge is something we buy that will lessen the detrimental impact to our NLV that would result from a movement against the dominant trend. To think of this in simpler terms, a hedge is a position in our portfolio that will increase in value when most of other positions in the portfolio are decreasing in value. Holding a bunch of long call positions while the market is pulling back can be an unpleasant, even hair-raising experience. Adding a hedge to your portfolio makes holding through the pullback more bearable.

Importantly, adding a hedge helps to smooth out fluctuations/ drawdowns in your NLV. As a trader, when you smooth out NLV fluctuations, you also smooth out your emotions. This reduces the likelihood that the emotional brain will take control of your trading, which in turn reduces the likelihood of you making detrimental trading decisions.

Think of a hedge as an insurance policy. It's not supposed to be fun. I just hold my nose and pay for it, much the same as I do when buying health insurance. Hedging isn't designed to make us money (although it certainly can!). It's designed to protect us from loss, just like insurance. Think of it as another business expense.

If I lose money on a hedge, there is no regret, no gnashing of teeth.

If I lose money on a hedge, I'm basically happy. In the same way I'm happy if I never have to make an insurance claim. If a hedge loses money, chances are most of the other positions in my portfolio are making money.

The question I normally get at this point is: "Wouldn't your portfolio performance be better if you didn't spend (waste) money on hedging?" This is like asking: "Wouldn't you be wealthier if you didn't waste money on health insurance?" The important thing to appreciate is we never **know** what the future holds, and hedging—like insurance—can shield us from adverse, unexpected events.

The main reason I hedge is to smooth out the fluctuations (i.e., falls) in my NLV, to try and prevent my 15 percent NLV stop-loss from ever being hit. As professional traders, we aren't trying to grow our account "as quickly as possible." Our goal is *sustainable* growth. The last thing on earth I want is to blow up my account. I also want to try and avoid a 15 percent fall in my NLV from its peak value. Hedging helps me to mitigate these risks. It helps to keep my trading less emotional and it reminds me that I must focus on the process of trading (rather than making money).

If you would like more information on hedging, I offer a detailed online video course on hedging, which is available to owners of this book at a discount. Head on over to https://taooftrading.com/bookbonus to check it out.

CHAPTER 13

THE PROCESS

"You do not rise to the level of your goals. You fall to the level of your systems."

—JAMES CLEAR

"You don't 'find' time to do what is important. You MAKE TIME. GO."

—JOCKO WILLINK

Money is, in some regards, a bit like the energy our bodies produce to live. We can't live without energy, just like we can't live without money. And if you don't have enough money right now, it's like not having enough energy.

In desiring more energy, you don't focus on obtaining more energy. No, you focus instead on what actions you should follow to become healthier, recognizing that a healthier body is a more energetic body. Am I sleeping enough? Am I getting enough exercise? What food should I eat for my nutrition? Am I managing my stress levels?

In trading, this means focusing on what actions will lead to better trading results, rather than focusing on "more money." These actions are what I refer to throughout this book as the process.

If you want to make money trading, don't focus on making money. Focus on the process, get really good at the process, enjoy the process, and the result will be trading profits.

You've heard me say this throughout the book, and you may be thinking: "Well, that's all well and good Simon, but what the heck *is* the process?"

I'm going to lay out my process for trading with you in detail in this chapter. Let's get started!

Here is a summary of the steps I go through. When trading, I:

1. Determine what phase the market is in.
2. Check for any significant economic reports or earnings announcements.
3. Review all existing open positions.
4. Hunt for new trades.
5. Refine the shortlist.
6. Select an appropriate option strategy.
7. Place the orders in the market.
8. Monitor my portfolio.

Let's go through each of these steps in more detail.

1. DETERMINE WHAT PHASE THE MARKET IS IN.

The first thing we want to do, before we even contemplate looking for trades to take, is determine whether the market is in a bull or bear phase. But before I do anything, I'll do four rounds of 4-7-8 breathing.

When I talk about "the market," what I'm really referring to is the S&P 500.

The S&P 500 index is the most important barometer of risk sentiment in the world and something every trader should be watching. The ticker symbol for the S&P 500 is SPX on most platforms. It is also important to be familiar with the ticker SPY, which is the SPDR S&P 500 ETF—the largest and most liquid ETF tracking the S&P 500.

As you know from chapter 5, the 200 SMA is the line in the sand between a bull market and a bear market. When the S&P 500 is trading above its 200 SMA, it is in a long-term uptrend. It will have periods of volatility, but our base-case working assumption is that the index will be inclined to work its way higher.

When the SPX is below its 200 SMA, it is in a long-term downtrend. Generally, it will be more volatile. Price movements—both up and down—will be more violent, media headlines will be more negative and scarier, and the market will have an overall "faster" feel to it.

However, as option traders, we are mostly concerned with the shorter-term market trend. Typically, I will hold an options position for anywhere from three days to four weeks. Some positions may be held for a longer or shorter period than this, but approximately 75 percent of my trades would fall within this duration. Given the shorter-term nature of options trading, we want to be more focused on the shorter-term moving averages. For the major indices, the two moving averages I focus on are the 8 EMA and the 21 EMA.

I consider the S&P 500 to be in a bull phase ("buy the dip") when:

- We have two (or more) consecutive closes above the 21 EMA
- The 8 EMA is above the 21 EMA

I consider the S&P to be in a bear phase ("sell the rip") when:

- We see two (or more) consecutive closes below the 21 EMA
- The 8 EMA is below the 21 EMA

Bull and Bear phases in SPY are highlighted in this chart.

If you think back to chapter 5, you'll recall that I use the 8 EMA and the 34 EMA to assess short-term trends for single stocks. Because single stocks tend to be more volatile than indices, I find the 8 EMA and the 34 EMA better time frames to use, compared with the 8 EMA and 21 EMA for indices.

Chart shows the 200 SMA acting as long-term support and resistance on the S&P 500.

When the index is in "buy the dip" mode (bull phase) I want to be focusing almost exclusively on long trades (buying calls and call debit spreads).

When the index is in short-term "sell the rip" mode (bear phase), I will usually want to have a hedge in place and be on the lookout for a bearish trade or two (buying puts or put debit spreads). Please note, this does NOT mean we are in a bear market! It just means short-term bearish trades are more likely to work than when the 8 EMA is below the 21 EMA on the S&P 500, and so we should focus on them a little more while the market remains in a bear phase.

When the market is in short-term "sell mode" I will wait for deeper pullbacks on potential bullish setups. For example, I'll wait for retracements to the 50 SMA rather than trying to buy at the 8 EMA or 21 EMA.

Avoid getting too bearish if the S&P is in short-term "sell mode" while it is above its 200 SMA. The index will often find support at the 34 EMA, 50 SMA, 100 SMA, or the 200 SMA, and once it has tested one of these levels, resume its long-term uptrend.

LET'S NOW MOVE TO A SCENARIO WHERE THE S&P 500 IS TRADING BELOW ITS 200 SMA.

The criteria for short-term "buy the dip" mode and "sell the rip" mode remain as per above, but the interpretation is slightly different.

"Buy the dip" mode when the index is below the 200 SMA means we can expect a countertrend rally that could last for a few days or even a few weeks. In this environment we want to be cautious about being 100 percent bearish in our trading portfolio and ensure we are taking some bullish trades. An underappreciated fact is that the sharpest and most aggressive rallies occur in bear markets, not bull markets, such is the power of a short-covering rally. We also want to watch carefully as the S&P 500 approaches its 200 SMA from below. This is often a major area of resistance where a bear market rally could fail. Of course, if the index pushes above the 200 SMA, we are transitioning back to a long-term bull market.

When the S&P 500 rallies up to the 200 SMA from below, the rally often stalls (see the shaded circles). Once it pushes through the 200 SMA, the uptrend continues.

When the market is in "sell mode" and the S&P 500 is below its 200 SMA, we really want to be focused on bearish trades. Buying puts and put debit spreads on rallies is the order of the day. Bullish trades are less likely to work well in this environment.

In addition to studying the S&P 500, I will also study the NASDAQ. Its ticker is NDX and **the ETF that tracks the NASDAQ is QQQ.**

The NASDAQ will often lead the S&P 500. If the NASDAQ makes new highs, expect the S&P to follow. It's almost as if the NASDAQ making new highs "gives permission" to the S&P 500 to do the same.

Other indices I follow on a daily basis are:

- The Russell 2000: this is a broad index covering 2,000 small and medium-sized US listed companies (small caps and mid-caps). **The ETF tracking the Russell 200 is IWM.**
- The Dow Jones Transportation Index: this is the most followed gauge of the American transportation sector. The "trannies" as this index is known, is often considered a leading indicator for the broader stock market. If manufacturing activity drops off, this is seen as a warning of slowing economic activity and potentially, a recession. In this environment, less goods are going to be shipped around and this will be revealed in the underperformance of transportation stocks. **The ticker for the ETF tracking the Dow Transports is IYT.**

2. CHECK FOR ANY SIGNIFICANT ECONOMIC REPORTS OR EARNINGS.

Each Monday I have a look at the economic calendar for the week at https://us.econoday.com/byweek.asp. If there are any significant events that week, such as the jobs report (first Friday of each month), or an FOMC interest rate decision, I can expect some additional volatility that day.

I will also check for any significant earnings announcements. Great places to check online for forthcoming earnings releases are https://earningswhispers.com/calendar and https://www.barchart.com/stocks/earnings-dividends.

3. REVIEW ALL EXISTING OPEN POSITIONS.

It's necessary to review all portfolio positions every day when the market is closed. That way, you have time and can do so in a more relaxed, less emotional manner. Don't be in a rush, take the time you need. With experience, this process will take only a few minutes each day.

Reviewing your positions while the market is open has some drawbacks:

- The values of your positions and your NLV will be jumping around in real time. This will be distracting and potentially stressful.
- If the market is undergoing a big move (particularly if that move is having a big effect on your NLV) you will be distracted and potentially impacted emotionally.

What I am looking for when I review my open positions is the following:

- Have any of my positions reached a stop-loss level (i.e., has their price fallen by 50 percent from my entry price, which is my mental stop-loss level)?
- Have any positions reached an area where I should start taking profit? When the underlying stock gets to +/- 2 ATRs from the mean, I will usually start to exit a position.
- Has the technical picture on any of my positions deteriorated? For example, if I am long calls on a stock whose price chart has started making a new lower low, I will consider exiting the position even if my 50 percent mental stop-loss hasn't been hit.
- Has my NLV fallen 15 percent from its most recent high value? If so, I will close all positions and go to cash for (at least) twenty-four hours.

Always stick to your stop-loss levels. Even if the stock does turn around and start going your way again, a re-entry is only a commission away...and commissions are virtually zero these days.

I like to do all of my analysis and preparation while the market is closed. This way when the market is open, I have a plan that I can stick to that was formulated while I was feeling unemotional about the market.

4. HUNT FOR NEW TRADES.

Now it's time to look for potential new trades.

There are many charting applications you can use for this purpose.

My preferred charting platform is Thinkorswim, which comes with my TD Ameritrade brokerage account. It's powerful, looks great, and has a reasonable learning curve. It has comprehensive scanning capability, and I have also developed a couple of custom indicators for the platform that make pinpointing trades easier. I really enjoy using the platform. Plus, it's free with a TD Ameritrade brokerage account.

Other charting platforms that I use (or have used in the past) and can recommend include:

- TradingView—Runs within your web browser and produces beautiful charts. Has a huge range of indicators and great drawing tools. Many of the charts in this book were produced using TradingView. Scanning capability is limited, however. It's well worth getting the Pro+ subscription. You can check it out at https://tradingview.com.
- StockCharts—If people are using TradingView for their charts, I usually recommend they complement that service with Stock-Charts for the scanning. StockCharts's actual charts are frankly not as good as some of the competition, but the scanning capability they offer is comprehensive and straightforward to use. TradingView + StockCharts is a great combination. Check it out at https://stockcharts.com/.
- TC2000—This is another capable charting platform that looks great. Good selection of indicators, but the drawing tools are a little more limited. Good scanning capability, but it comes with a bit of a learning curve. Check it out at www.TC2000.com.
- Trade Navigator—The interface on this software is old-fashioned but it produces great looking charts and has a strong selection of indictors and drawing tools available. It's one of

the few charting platforms I have used that can accommodate non-US stocks, so it's a great choice if that is important to you. It offers comprehensive scanning capability. The standard plan (which is all you need) is free with an active data service. Learn more at https://www.tradenavigator.com/products/comparison.

Scanning for trades is a massive timesaver. Instead of pouring over hundreds of charts each day, your charting platform can scan some basic criteria for you and provide a shortlist of stocks to add to your "weeding out" list. With practice, your trading can be done in as little as twenty minutes per day.

These are the criteria you will need to input into your charting platform of choice in order to scan for a shortlist:

BULLISH SETUP

Optionable stocks only	(We are options traders, after all)
Market capitalization >= $1 billion	(Small cap stocks can be too volatile)
Volume >= 500,000	(We want to trade stocks with reasonable liquidity)
8 EMA >= 21 EMA	(EMAs are stacked in a bullish fashion)
21 EMA >= 34 EMA	
34 EMA >= 55 EMA	
55 EMA >= 89 EMA	
Slow stochastics (8,3) <= 40	(The stock is in a pullback)
ADX (13) >= 20	(The stock is trending)

FOR ENTRY TRIGGER ONE, ADD THE FOLLOWING CRITERIA

RSI(2) yesterday <= 10
RSI(2) today > 10

FOR ENTRY TRIGGER TWO, ADD THE FOLLOWING CRITERIA

Close > Yesterday's High

Close > Open

BEARISH SETUP

Optionable stocks only

Market capitalization >= $1 billion

Volume >= 500,000

8 EMA <= 21 EMA	(EMAs are stacked in a bearish fashion)
21 EMA <= 34 EMA	
34 EMA <= 55 EMA	
55 EMA <= 89 EMA	
Slow stochastics (8,3) >= 60	(Stock has rallied within the downtrend)
ADX (13) >= 20	(Stock is trending)

FOR ENTRY TRIGGER ONE, ADD THE FOLLOWING CRITERIA

RSI(2) yesterday >= 90

RSI(2) today < 90

FOR ENTRY METHOD TWO, ADD THE FOLLOWING CRITERIA

Close < Yesterday's low

Close < Open

5. REFINE THE SHORTLIST.

After completing some bullish and bearish scans, it's time to complete the "weeding out" process. It's important to remember that scan results are only a starting point. Many of the stocks in the scan results will not be good candidates for trading. Just because they appear in the scan results does not give them any seal of endorsement as good trades. We have more work to do!

Here are the main criteria I like to analyze in the weeding out process:

1. Is the setup near support (for a bullish trade) or resistance (for a bearish trade)?
2. Can price move in my favor without running straight into significant support/resistance nearby?
3. Are there any very large gaps or candles near the setup?
4. Is the stock due to report earnings within the next two weeks?
5. Would this setup have produced profitable trades in the past?

I discussed each of these points in detail in chapter 10. Please refer to that chapter to review these points again.

At this point, I will print out the charts of the stocks I am looking to trade—in full color (my wife hates this!) and keep them for reference.

I will handwrite the reasons I like the trade on each chart. I keep all of my printed-out charts in two files—winners and losers. I find it helpful to go back and review trades I have taken in the past and review the winners and losers. By doing this regularly, you will over time develop a sixth sense or a "trader's brain" for what winning trades look like verse losing trades. I have found this practice to be invaluable in my trading.

Below is an example of one of my printed-out charts that goes into my trade diary. In this example, on October 17, 2019 I bought $65 calls in PSMT expiring on November 15, for $4.55 ($455 per contract). I sold them on October 28 for $7.60, **a gain of 85.4 percent in 11 days.**

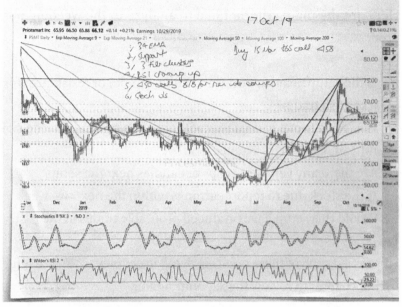

An example of one of my printed-out, hand-drawn-on charts.

I keep these printed charts, filed, and they form my trading diary. By reviewing them, I learn what is working for me and what isn't. I learn from my mistakes and over time, I am also able to track which stocks I seem to be "in sync" with. In doing so, I build a list of my favorite stocks to trade. I strongly recommend you follow this approach as it will help to greatly accelerate your progress as a trader.

6. SELECT AN APPROPRIATE OPTION STRATEGY.

Once I have a shortlist of the top one or two best-looking candidates for a Bounce 2.0 trade, I will decide on the option that I want to buy.

For bullish setups, I will be considering buying calls and call debit spreads and for bearish setups, I'll be looking at puts and put debit spreads.

When making the decision whether to buy naked options versus a debit spread, I'll take the following into consideration:

- The price of the options. For example, if I'm looking at a trade in stock with a high stock price (like AMZN, GOOGL, or BKNG) I will often trade a spread, so that I don't exceed my position size limits.
- If the options have a low price (e.g., $1.00 or less per contract) I'll nearly always buy naked options.
- My usual preference is to go with a debit spread, in order to reduce risk and my exposure to negative theta.

For naked option purchases, I will target options with a delta of around 70.

One other thing I want to check before committing to a trade is the option open interest. Open interest simply tells us how many options contracts are in existence. I do not want to be the only open interest in a contract! My rule of thumb is I want to see *at least* thirty open contracts (open interest of thirty) for every option contract I am looking to buy. For example, if I am considering buying three contracts, I want to see open interest of at least sixty contracts. An open interest of thirty contracts is the bare minimum; more is better. I won't trade an option with open interest of zero.

For a debit spread, my starting point is to buy an option with a delta of approximately 50 and then sell an option that will cover some of the extrinsic value I have paid on the delta 50 option.

Once I have settled on the option strategy I want to trade, I will write it down on my printed-out chart.

7. PLACE THE ORDERS IN THE MARKET.

The market is open and now we need to start working some orders.

There is an old saying that "amateurs open the market and professionals close it" and this saying is largely true. Consider that almost 30 percent of the day's volume on average is done in the last 30 minutes of trade!

The open is the most emotion-fueled period of the market session and it is full of punters buying stocks they just heard about on CNBC and retail traders panicking in and out of stocks as a result of fear or FOMO. But for a disciplined trader with a solid strategy and plan that they are committed to sticking to, the volatility of the open can provide some good opportunities.

A few words on how to execute a trade. When you look at the options chain in your brokerage platform, you will see all options have a "bid" price and an "ask" price.

The bid price is the price you will receive if you "hit the bid." To hit the bid is to place a sell order for an option for immediate execution. We never want to hit the bid when trading options.

The ask price is the price you will pay if you "hit the offer." Hitting the offer is placing a buy order for immediate execution. Again, we never want to hit the offer.

The difference between the bid and the ask is known as the spread. When placing options trades, ideally, we want to deal at "mid," which is the price midway between the bid and the ask. Hitting the bid or offer is also known as "crossing the spread" and is something we always want to avoid.

When trading highly liquid options like SPY or QQQ, the spread is usually only a couple of cents. In this case, dealing at mid is not much of a consideration. But for less liquid options, the spread can be significant. I have seen spreads $1 wide on $3–$4-dollar options. That's a 30 percent difference! You don't want to be paying half of this away to market makers if you don't have to. If you see an option with a spread of $3/$4, you want to try and pay $3.50 for the option. Don't hit the offer at $4!!

Now, let me try and save you some more money by telling you about a little trick that market makers often play to try and sucker traders into paying more for an option.

The trick goes something like this:

Let's say an option contract has a bid/ask spread of:

Bid $3.00	$4.00 Ask

You correctly assess that the midpoint of the spread is $3.50, so you place your buy order (your bid) at that level.

Now the market is:

Bid $3.50	$4.00 Ask

And then—within the blink of an eye, the $4.00 ask disappears and is replaced with an ask of $4.50!

Bid $3.50	$4.50 Ask

The underlying stock price hasn't moved, and so you think to yourself, "what the #$*% is going on?"

What is going on, is the market makers are trying to suck you into paying $4.50 for the option! These types of shenanigans happen all day every day. Please don't fall for them!

Hold fast with your bid at $3.50. If your order isn't filled within five minutes, increase your bid by $0.05. If it isn't filled after another five minutes, increase it by another $0.05. At this point, leave the order alone. Usually you will get filled. Sometimes your order won't get filled, but don't worry, there is always another bus to catch. And you are better off catching another trade than overpaying for this one.

If the market for an option is $3/$4 and you pay $4, you have just handed the market maker a much larger risk-free profit than they were expecting (or deserve). You have also just paid $4 for something that will be reflected in your portfolio with a value of $3.50 (at best). This is not great for your NLV!

So, when executing options trades, ALWAYS use limit orders and ALWAYS try to deal as close to the mid as possible.

8. MONITOR YOUR PORTFOLIO.

Any new positions that you have added to your portfolio need to be monitored daily. Ensure that you review your portfolio and your NLV as a whole. If you do suffer a 15 percent drawdown from your NLV's peak valuation, close all your positions and go to cash for twenty-four hours (at least). It's the pause that refreshes and will allow you to return to the markets feeling calmer and on a much more even keel emotionally.

PRO TIPS REGARDING THE PROCESS

1. Determine whether the market is in a bull swing (8 EMA > 21 EMA) or a bear swing (8 EMA < 21 EMA) and whether you want to have mostly bullish positions or mostly bearish positions in your portfolio.
2. Check for earnings releases or significant economic releases. Don't be surprised by volatility, know when to expect it.
3. Review all of your open positions. Are the original reasons you entered a trade still valid? Have any stop-loss levels been hit?
4. Perform some scans to get a shortlist of potential new trades.
5. Perform the weeding out process on your shortlist of potential trade candidates.
6. Determine the appropriate options strategy.
7. Always execute options trades as close to mid as possible and always use limit orders.
8. Monitor your new positions as well as your portfolio NLV on an ongoing basis.

CHAPTER 14

MAKING IT HAPPEN

"The only impossible journey is the one you never begin."

—ANTHONY ROBBINS

"What you can do, or dream you can, begin it. Boldness has a genius, power and magic in it."

—JOHANN WOLFGANG VON GOETHE

I have really put my heart and soul into this book, and I hope you have gotten value from it. I'm grateful to you for putting your trust in me by buying this book and I'm proud of you for getting this far. I am extremely confident that if you put what you have learned from this book into action, trading success will be in your future.

But taking action is KEY.

As much as l love and believe in trading, I'll be the first to admit that trading isn't for everyone. But the very fact that you have purchased and read this book is a great leading indicator that trading might just be the ticket for you.

The problem is, you won't *know* if trading is for you until you've given it a shot. It takes courage, discipline and a *lot* of repetition to become good enough to do this for a living. So, do yourself a favor and start small until you build up some consistency in your trading.

Also realize that trading is experiential. Learning about trading by reading a book is a lot like learning about swimming by reading a book. Both trading and swimming require complex execution skills. Reading helps greatly with the understanding...but not so much with the actual *doing*. The same can be said for learning to play golf, learning a musical instrument, or even learning to fly a plane.

If you have enjoyed this book and want to fast-track your development as a successful options trader, I am here to help. I run Tao of Trading, an online training education company, and you can find all details about the training courses I offer at http://taooftrading. com/. These additional resources could be exactly what you need to give you the confidence to take massive action towards accomplishing your trading goals.

In addition to this book, I am providing you with some fantastic online materials—either free or discounted—that you can access at https://taooftrading.com/bookbonus. I am offering these tools and discounts to you as a thank you for buying this book.

The online materials include:

· All of the options calculator spreadsheets you have seen in this book.
· Examples of the full-color chart setups that I use on various platforms.

- My "The Fibs Never Lie" online Fibonacci trading course, that will increase your ability to identify support, resistance, and high probability profit targets.
- My "How to Hedge" online course, which will teach you advanced risk management skills.
- My Tao of Trading "Options Academy," a comprehensive online video course that will teach you everything you need to know to become a professional options trader (this course includes the Bounce 2.0 setup, and teaches earnings setups, squeeze setups, and much more).

I am offering owners of this book a discount of $100 on any of my online video training courses.

"A real decision is measured by the fact that you've taken a new action. If there's no action, you haven't truly decided."

—ANTHONY ROBBINS

I now want to wrap up this chapter—and this book—by:

- Comparing and contrasting the attributes of winning versus struggling traders
- Discussing the importance of and offer advice on writing a trading plan
- Highlighting your possibilities as an options trader

WINNING VS. STRUGGLING TRADERS

Here's a cold, hard, fact of trading.

You can take two traders—Joe and Jane—who use the exact same trading method and have received the exact same training.

Jane is consistently profitable, while Joe is constantly donating money to the market.

How is this even possible?

Let's break it down by analyzing the common attributes of successful traders, as opposed to traders who struggle in the markets.

SUCCESSFUL TRADERS	STRUGGLING TRADERS
Keep it simple	Mistakenly think complexity leads to better outcomes
Find an edge and exploit their edge	Aren't even sure what an edge is
Enter and exit when their method tells them	Enter and exit when "their gut" tells them
Track their favorite instruments	Are always looking for something new to trade
Keep a diary and review their trades	Are oblivious to what's working for them and what isn't
Are 100% responsible and accountable for their results	Losing trades are never their fault
Understand probabilities	Take trading losses personally
Exercise emotional control	Aren't even consciously aware of their emotional state

SIMPLICITY

"Simplicity is the ultimate sophistication."

—LEONARDO DA VINCI

Often traders will start to screw up their own trading because either consciously or subconsciously, they think to themselves, "it can't be this easy." So, they add more indicators, or more rules, or start "tweaking" rules that work just fine, and in the process undo all the good that their simple trading method was doing for them.

EDGE

There is a very famous saying *"if you don't know what your edge is, you don't have one."* After reading this book, you now have several edges:

- You can identify a trend and the path of least resistance for a stock.
- You know whether you want to be bullish or bearish on a stock.
- You can identify high probability moments in time to join a trend.
- You know when a position isn't working and when you should take a stop-loss.
- You know where high probability profit targets exist.
- You know how to manage position size.
- You know how to manage portfolio risk.

Take a moment, right now, to quietly appreciate all that you have learned, and give yourself a big "high-five" for getting this far!

PLAN YOUR ENTRY AND EXIT

"Make time for planning: wars are won in the general's tent."
—STEPHEN COVEY

Never again enter a position in a stock because:

- The stock is rallying, and you're scared of missing out.
- Your brother-in-law said it's going to go up.
- "It just felt right."
- A friend or family member works at the company and they say it's great.
- You heard a convincing story on CNBC.

From now on, you are only going to enter a trade when you have an edge that you could clearly explain to me. This is the key to building profitability in your trading.

TRACKING YOUR FAVORITE INSTRUMENTS AND KEEPING A TRADING DIARY

If you track all of your trades, you will find over time that there are certain stocks that you trade well, over and over again. For example, I know for me personally, I have made more money trading Netflix and PayPal over the years than in any other stocks. When I see a setup in one of these stocks, I will always spend a little extra time analyzing it. Everybody's favorite stocks will be different and unique to them, but if you don't track all of your trades you will never be able to develop such a list.

As discussed in the previous chapter, I keep hard copies of my printed-out charts as my trading diary. You may prefer to keep a spreadsheet or a handwritten diary. It's up to you. I just find printing out my charts in color and writing on them is quite pleasurable, compared with keeping a spreadsheet.

100 PERCENT RESPONSIBILITY

"The hard reality of trading is that, if you want to create consistency, you have to start from the premise that no matter what the outcome, you are completely responsible."

—MARK DOUGLAS

You must be 100 percent responsible for your trading performance. Every trade you take is ultimately your own decision. To blame the market—or another person—for trading losses is incredibly disempowering for you. Not taking extreme ownership for your own trading performance will make your own improvement as a trader extremely difficult.

UNDERSTAND PROBABILITIES

"Consistent losers do almost everything to avoid accepting the reality that no matter how good a trade looks, it could lose."

—MARK DOUGLAS

You know from chapters 3 and 12 that, as traders, we are always dealing with probabilities, never a sure thing. We must leave deterministic thinking at the door and embrace probabilistic thinking. Embrace the uncertainty that exists in the markets because that's where all of the opportunities lie.

EMOTIONAL CONTROL

"The consistency you seek is in your mind, not in the markets."

—MARK DOUGLAS

"A memory without emotional charge is called wisdom."

DR. JOE DISPENZA

Happiness is peace in motion. Peace is happiness at rest.

Whatever you can do to improve your sense of peace in life will improve your trading results ten times more than a fancy, new indicator.

A significant step towards reducing stress and emotional swings in trading, is to write and follow a trading plan. I'm going to outline how to do that right now.

THE IMPORTANCE OF A TRADING PLAN

A trading plan is an iron-clad contract between yourself and you. Essentially it is a promise to yourself that you will follow certain guidelines in your trading to help maximize your consistency as a trader.

If you don't have a specific trading plan in place, there is a big risk that your trading will be aimless. A trade here, a trade there, have a stab at this trade...oh dear, that didn't work. You'll end up pushing and pushing to make things work until you just start donating your money to the market.

Traders without a trading plan often adopt a "video game mentality" to trading. They get distracted by the flashing indicators and the fast-moving numbers. Are those numbers even real? "Losing lives" in trading means you are bleeding real money out of your trading account. Please don't approach trading like a video game.

WRITING YOUR TRADING PLAN

Here are the key features of a good trading plan:

- Keep it simple.
- Get super clear on your "why."
- Define your approach.
- Define your edge.
- Position size appropriately.
- Enter and exit trades ONLY when your plan tells you to, not on the surges of emotion you feel during the market session.
- Manage your portfolio.
- Track your favorite instruments.
- Use familiar setups.
- Understand and accept probabilities.

KEEP IT SIMPLE

Your trading plan should be a simple document, the guts of which you can commit to memory. Two to three pages should suffice.

GET CRYSTAL CLEAR ON YOUR "WHY"

Know the answer to the question, "Why am I trading?" Is it to:

- Accelerate your wealth creation?
- Create a consistent source of supplementary income?
- Escape a full-time job you hate?
- Learn a new skill that will provide you with an income in retirement?
- Pay for children's/grandkids' education?
- Gain financial independence?

When you get really clear on your why, you can overcome all manner of obstacles. Write it down and internalize it.

DEFINE YOUR APPROACH

For example, you may decide upon an approach similar to this:

- I will have a technical approach to trading.
- I will follow the dominant trend and buy a reversion to the mean on the daily chart.
- I will ignore "hot tips."
- While I may listen to the opinions of others, I will ALWAYS make MY OWN decisions.
- I will focus on swing trading stocks that are in sympathy with the dominant trend of the overall market.

DEFINE YOUR EDGE

For example:

- I am only going to take trades on a Bounce 2.0 setup.
- If there is no Bounce 2.0 setup, there is no trade.

POSITION SIZE APPROPRIATELY

Commit to the maximum amount of risk you are prepared to take on a single position and never, ever exceed this. If you have a small account and want to grow it aggressively, I would suggest that 10 percent of your NLV be the maximum allowable amount of risk you could take on a single position. Only ever enter a position in 5 percent (max) increments.

If you have a "large" account, the more conventional "don't risk more than 1 to 2 percent of your account on any single trade" guidelines may be more appropriate.

ENTRIES AND EXITS

Have a list of agreements with yourself about precisely how and when you will enter and exit trades. For example:

- I will only enter a trade when all of the Bounce 2.0 trade criteria are met, and I get an entry trigger from either RSI(2) and/or price action.
- I will only enter 50 percent of my maximum trade size initially. If I buy on a pullback to the 34 EMA or 50 SMA, I will add to my position after the stock closes above its 21 EMA.
- I will immediately cut any options position where the premium is worth 50 percent of my entry price.
- I will cut any position when the trend I was expecting is looking questionable, either because price has made a new lower low (in the case of an uptrend) or new higher high (in the case of a downtrend).

MANAGE YOUR PORTFOLIO RISK

If you have a 10 percent NLV limit per position, you can hold a maximum of ten positions. But don't have ten tech stocks. Don't have ten long naked call option positions. Diversify your trades across sectors and strategies.

Always trade within your means or beneath your means. Trading beneath your means is trading smaller than your maximum risk budget would allow. This is great advice for beginning traders and it is what you must do if your position size is freaking you out. You know your position size is freaking you out if you are finding trading stressful and you are finding it difficult to honor your stop-losses. This is a sure sign you need to reduce your position size.

TRACK YOUR FAVORITE INSTRUMENTS

I have met so many traders whose trading journey ends up looking something like this:

- One month they're trading stocks ("we're in a bull market, man!")
- When that didn't work out, they jump to options ("strangles and spreads, that's where it's at, baby!")
- When that didn't work out, they jump to forex ("I just bought this forex robot, it does all the trading for me!")
- When that inevitably didn't work out, they jump onto Bitcoin ("it's gonna replace money!")
- When that didn't work out, they jump on social media ("I saw this ad on Facebook about trading binary options...")

By now, they have to go back to work, because they have blown up whatever trading capital they had left.

You now have in your possession a winning system for trading options.

Stick with it.

Start building watchlists of your favorite stocks.

Get to know the top five or six stocks in each of the major S&P sectors.

After a few hundred trades, names will start to become familiar as stocks that work for YOU. Commit to developing and building upon the knowledge you have gained in this book.

UNDERSTAND AND ACCEPT PROBABILITIES

Realize that even the best-looking setups can (and will) lose money. Even when you feel convinced that something is going to happen, understand and accept ahead of time that it may not. It's often those setups that you feel so confident about that you want to bet the farm on them, that hurt you the most. Trading success is not about being right, it's about being prepared for anything and managing risk.

If you don't understand and accept probabilities, you will take trading losses personally. This is a bad, bad, road to go down as it leads to frustration, fear, revenge trading, and your executive brain ceding control to your emotions.

HOW TO KNOW IF YOU'RE ON THE WRONG TRACK

Can you relate to any of these feelings?

- "OMG this stock has moved against me for ANOTHER day! Should I cut my losses now? Crap, I should have done that three days ago! Surely the stock CAN'T go any lower? Maybe I'll just hang on and wait for it to turn around?"
- "Should I take profit here? Maybe this run is only just getting

started? That girl on CNBC sounded very bullish! But if I don't sell, what if it falls below my entry price? What should I do?"
- "Dang, the stock has just gone below my entry level. Should I add to my position? Should I cut my position?"

A good trading plan is designed to get rid of all these types of feelings. If you EVER have feelings like these, either you are not following your trading plan, or you don't have one.

When amateurs get into a trade, they basically close their eyes and hope that markets move in their favor. They sweat when the market moves even a little bit against them and they're constantly plagued by indecision. "Should I cut?" "Should I take profits?" Should I add to my position?" "When will the market turn around?!" Hope has no place in trading. Focus on your process and stick to your stops.

Professionals realize that successful trading largely comes down to maintaining a calm, decisive state of mind while trading. Amateurs are never going to be consistently profitable until they can achieve that state of mind. Following a good trading plan can help you to develop and retain the right state of mind.

WHAT ARE THE POSSIBILITIES WITH OPTION TRADING?

I do not want you to be focused on how much money you think you are going to make on each trade. But understanding what your overall goals are as an options trader is important.

I encourage you to think of your objectives in terms of a specific goal, like:

- "I want to grow my account to $X"; or
- "I want to generate $Y in income, per month"

Let's say you have set yourself a target and you want to achieve a return on your portfolio of 2.5 percent per week.

"Don't be ridiculous, 2.5 percent per WEEK? That's not even possible!"

Let's have a look at what you would need to do, in order to achieve this type of return.

Assume you have a $10,000 account, and you are going to risk 5 percent of your NLV on average, per trade.

If you were to close out one trade per week, at a 50 percent profit, your returns would look like this:

Trade size	$500
Return (%)	50%
Return ($)	$250
Return (% of $10k portfolio)	2.5%

What if you closed five trades per week, with three of them winners and two of them losers (for a 60 percent win rate)?

Winning Trades	$750 profit	(three winners @ $250 profit per trade)
Losing Trades	$500 loss	(two losers @ $250 loss per trade)
Net Return ($)	$250	
Net Return (%)	2.5%	

The outcome would be the same. You would achieve a return of 2.5 percent per week. And this is assuming that your winning and losing trades are the same size.

So, maybe 2.5 percent per week is an achievable goal?

But what would that actually mean for you as an options trader?

When you're compounding returns on a weekly basis (rather than on an annual basis), compounding really does start to look interesting! If you were able to consistently achieve a return of 2.5 percent per week and kept compounding your returns, this is how your $10,000 account would look after one year:

STARTING BALANCE		$10,000.00	
WEEKLY RETURN		**2.5%**	
END OF WEEK	**ACCOUNT BALANCE**	**END OF WEEK**	**ACCOUNT BALANCE**
1	$10,250.00	27	$19,478.00
2	$10,506.25	28	$19,964.95
3	$10,768.91	29	$20,464.07
4	$11.038.13	30	$20,975.68
5	$11,314.08	31	$21,500.07
6	$11,596.93	32	$22,037.57
7	$11,886.86	33	$22,588.51
8	$12,184.03	34	$23,153.22
9	$12,488.63	35	$23,732.05
10	$12,800.85	36	$24,325.35
11	$13,120.87	37	$24,933.49
12	$13,448.89	38	$25,556.82
13	$13,785.11	39	$26,195.74
14	$14,129.74	40	$26,850.64
15	$14,482.98	41	$27,521.90
16	$14,845.06	42	$28,209.95
17	$15,216.18	43	$28,915.20
18	$15,596.59	44	$29,638.08
19	$15,986.50	45	$30,379.03
20	$16,386.16	46	$31,138.51
21	$16,795.82	47	$31,916.97
22	$17,215.71	48	$32,714.90
23	$17,646.11	49	$33,532.77
24	$18,087.26	50	$34,371.09
25	$18,539.44	51	$35,230.36
26	$19,002.93	**52**	**$36,111.12**

Your $10,000 would be worth $36,111.12, for an effective annual rate of return of over 360 percent. That's somewhat better than the 10 percent Wall Street was offering, isn't it?

As you know, this profession is called "trading," not "guaranteed income," so there are no guarantees that you will achieve returns anything like these. But I hope that this exercise highlights just what is possible without taking excessive amounts of risk, and that this motivates you to continue your trading journey.

FINAL THOUGHTS

Finishing this book fills me with a sense of accomplishment. When I set out to write this book, I realized that there are already many books on option trading available. However, many of them are quite boring to read and difficult to understand. Many of the options books available are books someone would only read if either their boss made them read it, or it was required to pass an exam (I have firsthand experience with both scenarios!).

In writing this book, my main goal was to write a book on options trading that was both simple and engaging. I wanted to give you, the reader, all the really important information you need to become a successful options trader but do it in a manner that was light-hearted and enjoyable. I feel that I have achieved those objectives... hopefully you agree!

There are many other trading setups that I use and teach, but the Bounce 2.0 setup is one of the easiest and most intuitive to pick up, hence my decision to include it in this book. It also represents the bread-and-butter of my trend continuation trading.

If you would like to deepen your trading education with more advanced techniques—Squeeze trades, earnings trades, hedging strategies, and much more—please pay me a visit at my main website https://taooftrading.com.

It is my sincere hope that after reading this book, you will have the confidence and the know-how to trade the markets successfully using one of my favorite proven setups. You will be light years ahead of other traders who don't know or appreciate the importance of factors like emotional control and managing risk.

Don't forget to check out the bonuses I have prepared for you at https://taooftrading.com/bookbonus. I hope you enjoy and make good use of them.

My firm belief is that the knowledge and wisdom I have shared in this book can help take your trading to the next level and I wish you all the best on your trading journey. I love the heck out of all traders, because we are all doing—or aspiring to do—something that most people say can't be done. It takes courage to fly in the face of conventional wisdom. May this book give you the wings to do so.

"You're not going to find happiness. You have to make it. So, get out there and make some happiness."

—JOCKO WILLINK

Simon Ree
January 2020

ABOUT THE AUTHOR

SIMON REE has been an active trader and investor since 1992 and a financial-markets professional since 1996. He previously held senior positions with Goldman Sachs in Sydney and Citibank in Singapore before deciding to focus on options trading full-time in 2017. Simon's professional career spans more than twenty-five years in the private-banking and investment-banking industries, including work with major global investment banks. Simon has worked on both the markets side and the relationship-management side of the banking industry. He has a very strong background in capital markets across all the major asset classes and developed a particular expertise in equity options.

During his time at Goldman Sachs, Simon founded and headed the Markets Desk for Australasia. His team was responsible for credit, foreign exchange, and over-the-counter derivatives transactions. While at Citibank, Simon worked and consulted with some of the wealthiest and most successful families across Australia and Southeast Asia. He helped hundreds of people across this region learn how to trade profitably and build wealth.

Simon has spent well over 20,000 hours watching and analyzing markets throughout his career. The depth of his trading knowledge and his robust banking-industry experience helped him "crack the code" of how to trade safely and profitably. He has a passion for teaching others what he has learned about the markets and profitable trading.

In addition to trading, Simon is passionate about helping people unlock their full human potential. He is a certified Jeet Kune Do instructor and Reiki master. He resides in Singapore with his family, where he works as an options trader, a trading coach/mentor, a consultant, and a public speaker.

DISCLAIMER

Important! By reading this book you explicitly agree to all of the following.

DISCLOSURE: The author of this book, together with Tao of Trading Ltd, its managers, employees, and affiliates (collectively "The Company") do not make any guarantee or warranty about what returns the reader can expect from their investment and trading results.

The Company is not affiliated with, nor does it receive compensation from, any specific security.

The Company is not registered or licensed by any governing body in any jurisdiction to give investing or trading advice or provide investment or trading recommendations.

ALWAYS DO YOUR OWN RESEARCH and consult with a licensed investment professional before making an investment or trade. This book and associated online and electronic material should not be used as a basis for making any investment or trade.

The past performance of any trading system or methodology is not necessarily indicative of future results.

CFTC RULE 4.41 – HYPOTHETICAL OR SIMULATED PERFOR-MANCE RESULTS HAVE CERTAIN LIMITATIONS. UNLIKE AN ACTUAL PERFORMANCE RECORD, SIMULATED RESULTS DO NOT REPRESENT ACTUAL TRADING. ALSO, SINCE THE TRADES HAVE NOT BEEN EXECUTED, THE RESULTS MAY HAVE UNDER-OR-OVER COMPENSATED FOR THE IMPACT, IF ANY, OF CERTAIN MARKET FACTORS, SUCH AS LACK OF LIQUIDITY.

SIMULATED TRADING PROGRAMS IN GENERAL ARE ALSO SUBJECT TO THE FACT THAT THEY ARE DESIGNED WITH THE BENEFIT OF HINDSIGHT. NO REPRESENTATION IS BEING MADE THAT ANY ACCOUNT WILL OR IS LIKELY TO ACHIEVE PROFIT OR LOSSES SIMILAR TO THOSE SHOWN.

All trades, patterns, charts, systems, etc., discussed in this book and associated online and electronic material are for illustrative purposes only and not to be construed as specific advisory recommendations.

All ideas, opinions, and material presented are entirely those of the author and do not necessarily reflect those of the publisher.

No system or methodology has ever been developed that can guarantee profits or ensure freedom from losses. No representation or implication is being made that using the methodology or system will generate profits or ensure freedom from losses.

Made in United States
Orlando, FL
20 September 2024

51718879R00211